W9-ABN-229

POLITICAL REALITIES
Edited on behalf of the Politics Association by
Derek Heater

Comparative
Government

Roger Charlton

VERNON REGIONAL
JUNIOR COLLEGE LIBRARY

Longman
London and New York

LONGMAN GROUP UK LIMITED
*Longman House, Burnt Mill, Harlow, Essex CM20 2JE, England
and Associated Companies throughout the World.*

Published in the United States of America
by Longman Inc., New York.

© Longman Group UK Limited 1986
*All rights reserved; no part of this publication
may be reproduced, stored in a retrieval system,
or transmitted in any form or by any means, electronic,
mechanical, photocopying, recording, or otherwise,
without the prior written permission of the Publishers.*

First published 1986

ISBN 0 582 35395 5

*Set in 10/12pt Times Roman, Linotron 202
Produced by Longman Group (F.E.) Ltd
Printed in Hong Kong*

British Library Cataloguing in Publication Data

Charlton, Roger
  Comparative government. — (Political realities)
  1. Comparative government
  I. Title   II. Series
  320.3   JF51
  ISBN 0-582-35395-5

Library of Congress Cataloging-in-Publication Data

Charlton, Roger.
  Comparative government.
  (Political realities)
  Bibliography: p.
  Includes index.
  1. Comparative government.   I. Title.   II. Series.
JF51.C43 1986   320.3   85-23670
ISBN 0-582-35395-5

Contents

Political Realities:
the nature of the series

A great need is felt for short books which can supplement or even replace textbooks and which can deal in an objective but realistic way with problems that arouse political controversy. The series aims to break from a purely descriptive and institutional approach to one that will show how and why there are different interpretations both of how things work and how they ought to work. Too often in the past 'British Constitution' has been taught quite apart from any knowledge of the actual political conflicts which institutions strive to contain. So the Politics Association sponsors this series because it believes that a specifically civic education is an essential part of any liberal or general education, but that respect for political rules and an active citizenship can only be encouraged by helping pupils, students and young voters to discover what the main objects are of political controversy, the varying views about the nature of the constitution – themselves often highly political – and what the most widely canvassed alternative policies are in their society. From such a realistic appreciation of differences and conflicts reasoning can then follow about the common processes of containing or resolving them peacefully.

The specific topics chosen are based on an analysis of the main elements in existing A level syllabuses, and the manner in which they are treated is based on the conviction of the editor that almost every examination board is moving, slowly but surely, away from a concentration on constitutional rules and towards a more difficult but important concept of a realistic political education or the enhancement of political literacy.

This approach has, of course, been common enough in the universities for many years. Quite apart from its civic importance, the teaching of politics in schools has tended to lag behind university practice and expectations. So the editor has aimed to draw on the most up-to-date academic knowledge, with some of the books being written by university teachers, some by secondary or further education teachers, but each aware of the skills and knowledge of the other.

The Politics Association and the editor are conscious of the great importance of other levels of education, and are actively pursuing studies and projects of curriculum development in several directions, particularly towards CSE needs; but it was decided to begin with A level and new developments in sixth form courses precisely because of the great overlap here between teaching in secondary school and further education colleges, whether specifically for examinations or not; indeed most of the books will be equally useful for general studies.

Derek Heater

Preface

This book seeks to introduce the subject of comparative politics to students who have only recently begun the academic study of politics. Of necessity, its coverage of such a vast field is highly selective. In particular the chosen emphasis on regimes – ruling individuals and groups and governing institutions – focuses attention mainly on political decision-makers, and away from the political behaviour of the general populace. From a comparative perspective this emphasis is readily justifiable. In all of the world's regimes these key personnel comprise only a very small percentage of the total population. In most contemporary regimes the political impact of the mass of the population is very limited. In many it is negligible.

I would like to record here two debts that I can never adequately repay. The first is to the late Michael Croft who introduced me to the study of comparative politics. The second is to Bernard Crick for assistance, both academic and practical, over many years. In writing and re-writing this book I have been greatly helped, albeit in very different ways, by two colleagues, Ellen Graham and Ronald Kaye. Derek Heater has been a very patient and very helpful editor. Above all, I would like to thank my wife, Jacqueline, for encouragement, support, and an enormous amount of very practical assistance. Finally, the book is dedicated to my mother, in the hope that it will have one uncritical reader.

Figures and Tables

1 Contemporary Regimes:
An Introductory Classification

In January 1984, the membership of the United Nations stood at 158. This figure gives a useful, but only very approximate, indication of the total number of states in the contemporary world: that is, defined territories whose independence is internationally recognised through the right to enter into diplomatic relations with other states. The true figure is, in fact, closer to 170, since four major states (North and South Korea, Switzerland and Taiwan) are not currently members of the UN, and a number of mini-states are also not included in its membership. Curiously one state, the Union of Soviet Socialist Republics, has, in effect, three memberships, since two of its constituent republics, the Belorussian and the Ukrainian, are members in their own right.

These 170 independent states, varying vastly in size, population, resources, and wealth, collectively and individually comprise the subject matter for the study of comparative politics. Politically each one of these countries is in many ways unique, but each one also exhibits some recurrent features. It is on these identifiable recurrent features that the subject of comparative politics seeks to build; aiming explicitly to identify, and to underline, significant similarities of structure and operation among different countries.

States and constitutions

Inevitably, such similarities must initially be sought at a very general level. A very convenient starting point is to take a broad historical perspective on the development of the contemporary international system of states. From such a perspective, the crucial factor is the seemingly inexorable spread over the past three centuries of the idea and the practice of the independent

1

nation-state outwards from Europe to the rest of the world, which had hitherto developed other forms of political organisation. The culmination of these developments came in the aftermath of the Second World War when Western empires were rapidly dismantled and membership of the United Nations rose swiftly from its original level of 51 in 1945. Virtually all of the newly independent states were duly provided with that most important of birth certificates, a constitution.

In all constitutions the bulk of the document, usually well over half, deals with organisational and institutional matters. All states require some sort of an 'organisational map' to provide a detailed description of the various governmental institutions and offices as well as the procedures to be followed by individuals and groups in achieving their goals properly and legally. Moreover the institutional parameters within which such codes can vary are determined by the surprisingly limited number of political structures and institutions available to date. Apart from political parties, and with the partial exception of federalism, which in its modern, centralised, form dates from the late 18th century, there are in practice no distinctively modern political institutions. All the other institutions which exist in modern states are adapted from pre-modern and traditional political systems, where executives, civilian and military bureaucracies, judiciaries and legislative assemblies were already well developed.

Given this limited institutional choice it is not surprising that, despite many differences, virtually all constitutions exhibit one basic institutional similarity. They provide for the separation of legislative, executive and judicial institutions by stipulating that laws will be made by legislatures, that executives will put these laws into effect, while judiciaries are empowered to resolve any resultant disputes. With the partial exception of Taiwan this institutional tripartism is to be found in all constitutional texts, whether European, African, Asian, or Latin American. The outcome has been that the legislatures, bureaucracies and courts so familiar to the Western world have become world-wide political phenomena. Similar circumstances have, in turn, ensured the world-wide existence of equally familiar political parties and pressure groups. The spread of independent nationhood and its attendant constitution-making have therefore ensured that the key institutions of modern government have been transported and transferred across the globe in the post-war years as an integral part of the development of a world of politically independent states. Nevertheless, the institutional variations between different states are also large. In particular, one of the most obvious features of even a brief overview of political activity in contemporary states is the extent to which different states utilise and combine, ignore or discard, specific institutions or institutional combinations.

Many of these political variations will not be recorded in the relevant constitution. Comparative politics, therefore, cannot simply be the comparative study of constitutions. In the first place, at any one time, a substantial number of the constitutions of the world's states will either be in full or partial suspension or in the process of being rewritten. In the second place, no single document, however frequently amended, could ever definitively hope to provide what has been variously termed a 'power map' or an 'autobiography of power distribution', for a specific society.[1] Constitutions, by definition, cover only the legally codified structures and processes of government and politics – a purview which can conveniently be described as the formal political institutions and interactions of the state. Constitutions are becoming longer and more complex, seeking to incorporate and regulate institutional arrangements such as party systems and pressure groups which were ignored by their nineteenth-century counterparts. Even so, there is always a gap between constitutional promise and political realities. This gap reflects the existence and impact of what may be termed informal and uncodified forces, arrangements and interactions. Such a gap is always present, although its precise nature and extent varies widely from country to country. Thus, on the one hand, 'in each state there is a set of political institutions without which the state in its present form could not persist.'[2] On the other hand, it is equally important to stress that states also vary very widely in the extent to which the significance of these key or basic institutions is truly reflected in the formal, written constitution.

Regimes

Taken by themselves, the formal written constitutions of the world's states are likely to offer useful, but limited, opportunities for the identification of politically important similarities and differences, on which to base a classification of these states. The study of comparative politics must therefore also encompass those informal, but nonetheless crucial structures, arrangements and procedures which affect the ways in which political power is achieved and held, political decisions made and policies implemented in any state. This combination of the formal and the informal, of written and unwritten rules, institutions and practices is commonly called a regime. All states possess some form of political regime. All regimes, in turn, are composed of a combination of governing individuals and governing institutions. Thus, governments comprise those individuals and groups who occupy and control the central political institutions – legislatives and executives – in a state. Both these central institutions and their occupants form key components of the regime – as do bureaucracies, judiciaries, parties and pressure groups.

One result of this interaction between formal rules and informal pressures in individual regimes is that superficially similar political structures and institutions may in practice have very different political functions and effects, and therefore operate in very different ways in different states. Consequently, the overall political importance and impact of individual political institutions, as well as the groups and individuals who occupy and control these institutions, will also be found to vary widely from regime to regime. Ultimately, these variations could be said to be as numerous as the world's regimes. For each state possesses a distinctive 'political culture'. This is an amalgam of the political values, beliefs and attitudes of its members, which is developed through that state's unique, historical experiences. This political culture will, in turn, leave its mark on the operation of all political institutions and processes. Consequently, each state will be found to have certain characteristic ways of operating politically, as a result of this unique and unrepeatable blend of historical legacies and contemporary institutions, practices and beliefs.

Nevertheless, if a different perspective is adopted and broad similarities between and among regimes are consciously sought, an appreciation of the uniqueness of each state's practices and experiences will be tempered by a recognition of the extent to which these same regimes fall, both deliberately and accidentally, into certain identifiable political patterns common to a number of different regimes. These patterns are formed by some combination of similar (but not identical) historical experiences, similar (but not identical) types of current political behaviour, and similar (but not identical) aims and aspirations for the future. This book is concerned to identify and illustrate these patterns only in the broadest and most general sense. Inevitably, its brief and selective global coverage of contemporary political institutions and practices can do little more than point the way to more detailed and more comprehensive analyses.

Indeed it is currently impossible to present any detailed and definitive classification which would unambiguously pigeonhole every contemporary state and regime. The reasons for this are a continuing paucity of easily accessible information about many contemporary states and the rapidity with which some states change from one regime type to another. Nonetheless it is possible to identify three broad political patterns into one of which *most* of the world's 170 regimes can fairly straightforwardly be fitted. The first of these regime patterns is formed by identifying those regimes which are politically and economically competitive. These regimes are mainly (but by no means exclusively) to be found in the advanced industrial societies of the capitalist West, and can be termed the First World pattern. This pattern forms a marked contrast to the centrally planned and (broadly) one-party regimes of the communist Second World, formed by an 'Eastern bloc' of (mainly) industrialised states. Similar marked contrasts exist between these two patterns and the third pattern of regimes formed by the (mainly) economically and politically underdeveloped states of the Third World, or, to use the currently fashionable term, the 'South'.

First World regimes. There has been a large measure of agreement in recent years over the approximately thirty states which are widely accepted as being stable and competitive liberal democracies or pluralist political systems. (Due to lack of information, analyses have always excluded 'microstates' with less than one million inhabitants. Some of these microstates, such as Iceland, are clearly democracies). In recent years there have

Table 1.1   Contemporary democracies

States defined as democracies in five recent studies		States defined as democracies in four of five recent studies
Australia	Japan	Ceylon (Sri Lanka)
Austria	The Netherlands	Chile
Belgium	New Zealand	Greece
Canada	Norway	Jamaica
Costa Rica	Sweden	The Philippines
Denmark	Switzerland	Turkey
Finland	The United Kingdom	Uruguay
France	The United States	Venezuela
West Germany		
India	*Total* 21	*Total* 8
Ireland		
Israel		
Italy		

Source: G. Bingham Powell, Jr, *Contemporary Democracies* (Harvard University Press, 1982), p 5.

been five scholarly studies which have sought to identify contemporary democratic regimes, and 21 countries have appeared in all five lists.[3] These 21 states are listed in Table 1.1. Eight further states appear in four out of the five lists and can therefore be safely assumed to be genuine contemporary democracies too. However these additions (again listed in Table 1.1) immediately underline the problems involved in attempting classifications of this type. Indeed, only about twenty of these regimes operated continuously in a democratic manner between the years 1958 and 1985. In the rest democracy was at some time within this period either suspended, or, in some cases, completely replaced by a dictatorship.

Even states which have exhibited relatively long histories of democracy have not proved immune from political breakdown and collapse, and, particularly from that commonest of modern forms of instability, the military coup. The example of France in 1958 neatly underlines this. Here a successful military coup paved the way for the transition from the Fourth to the Fifth Republic. Moreover, that commonest of modern forms of authoritarian or dictatorial rule, namely military government, has occurred, and in some cases continues to occur, in a number of these 'contemporary democracies'. Clearly in a number of states the roots of democracy lie very close to the surface. Thus, Greece was under military rule between 1967 and 1974. In Turkey, the military has intervened persistently and, at regular intervals, has taken control of government. Chile and Uruguay remained under military dictatorship continuously between 1973 and 1985. Other states widely identified as 'democracies' may have escaped military rule, but periods of widespread political violence and subsequent emergency rule have severely tested democratic rule in India, Jamaica and Sri Lanka. In the Philippines democratic rule disappeared under a civilian dictatorship from 1972 to 1986.

Consequently, making lists of democracies may seem to be a somewhat frustrating exercise, but it is important to stress that in approximately twenty states stable and competitive regimes have existed continuously over recent decades. Moreover, at any one time, democratic regimes are likely to exist in at least ten other states, although the specific states involved will vary quite markedly, often over relatively short periods of time. Thus, the late 1970s saw the restoration of competitive party systems in two European states, Portugal and Spain, which had long histories of authoritarian and undemocratic rule, as well as in two African military regimes, Ghana and Nigeria. Significantly, by 1984 the two African experiments with competitive democracy had succumbed once again to military rule, whilst the two European experiments continued, albeit not without traumas, particularly in Spain where the armed forces pose a major threat to the continuation of democratic rule.

This reveals a wider point. Most of the hard core of democracies – states with long histories of democratic competition and of political stability – are in the economically developed First World; a glance at the list of 21 states unanimously accepted as democracies in Table 1.1 underlines this. On this listing only Costa Rica, India and Israel remain as potential examples of democracy among Third World states. Conversely, a large part of the shifting group of 'temporary' democracies is comprised of varying permutations of Third World states. This highlights the point that free and competitive politics has much less deep historical roots and faces many more pressing challenges among the economically weaker states of the South. Consequently, whilst the number of states has steadily risen as progressively more and more states have been created in the wake of the break-up of the European empires, the number of democracies has not risen proportionately. G Bingham Powell points out that there were approximately 22 democracies among 64 independent states in 1920, and yet only 29 democracies among 121 states by 1960.[4]

However, at any one time over recent decades, a group of about thirty states, situated mainly but not exclusively in the industrialised North Atlantic region has espoused the ideology of liberal-democracy. This same group of states has consistently practised open political competition for the highest offices of state. In these states a number of institutionalised (organised) political parties freely and fairly compete for political power through elections in which most citizens are able to participate. These elections occur without major disruptions and upheavals even if political power changes hands. Between elections organised non-governmental pressure groups openly compete to influence power-holders. In these states, distinct – if variable and moveable – boundaries are maintained between state and society. Normally a substantial private sector in the economy is maintained. However, it is not the size of this private sector which is most significant. What is most important is that clear distinctions continue to be recognised between state institutions and non-state or social institutions, such as the press and the trade unions, and that these are accorded some degree of political independence. Above all, the essential hallmark of these competitive or pluralistic democracies is that they allow open political competition and opposition between organised political parties for all important political offices, as well as extensive public participation through free elections and through the free play of group activity.

Second World regimes. There exists a second easily identifiable and reasonably politically homogeneous group of states which is also situated mainly (but not exclusively) in the industrialised North of the globe, and which comprises the world's Marxist governments or communist regimes. Sixteen regimes currently form the core of this group, but arguably twice this number could be included, or more if the fifty or so contemporary states which have publicly espoused some form of socialism and have copied some of the institutional features of the communist states are also counted. This increasingly confused picture stems from the fact that in recent years a number of Third World states, mainly but not exclusively in Africa, have not only identified themselves with Marxism-Leninism but have also in many cases acquired two other key hallmarks of this group of states in their establishment of single ruling parties and substantial measures of state ownership in their economies.

Consequently, as can be seen from Table 1.2 below, lists of contemporary communist regimes differ widely in length

Table 1.2 *Contemporary communist states: two lists*

Afghanistan	Madagascar	Albania
Albania	Mongolia	Bulgaria
Angola	Mozambique	China
Benin	Poland	Cuba
Bulgaria	Romania	Czechoslovakia
China	San Marino	German Democratic
Congo	Somalia	Republic
Cuba	USSR	Hungary
Czechoslovakia	Vietnam	Kampuchea
Ethiopia	South Yemen	North Korea
German Democratic	Yugoslavia	Laos
Republic		Mongolia
Guinea-Bissau and	*Total* 28	Poland
Cape Verde (2)		Romania
Hungary		USSR
Kampuchea		Vietnam
North Korea		Yugoslavia
Laos		*Total* 16

Source: Bogdan Szajkowski, ed, *Marxist Governments: A World Survey* 3 vols, (Macmillan, 1981)

Source: Stephen White, John Gardner & George Schöpflin, *Communist Political Systems: An Introduction* (Macmillan, 1982), Table 1:1, p 2.

according to the strictness of the criteria demanded. At their most generous, some analysts would accept simple 'self-ascription', maintaining that a commitment to Marxism is a sufficient defining feature.[5] Other analysts have underlined the weakness of using this as the main criterion. Certainly self-ascription is not normally used to define any other groups of regimes. For example the United Nations, shortly after its formation, asked its member states how their regimes were to be described, and found that the overwhelming response (reality notwithstanding) was 'democratic'.[6] Consequently, other comparativists have sought further and stricter criteria to distinguish the sixteen older, firmly established communist or Marxist-Leninist regimes from their more recently established, and often transient, emulators in the Third World.

A recent introductory textbook, covering the sixteen states which in the 1980s could be classified unambiguously as communist, highlights three major differences between the communist states and the Western liberal-democratic states and argues that 'together these features may be regarded as the defining characteristics of a communist state.' In the first place, all the communist states have adopted Marxism-Leninism as an official ideology and as the basis of the legitimacy (moral right to rule) of their rulers. Second, in contrast to the predominantly 'market' economies of the regimes of the capitalist states, the communist states have a 'command' economy, which is centrally planned and publicly rather than privately owned. Third, these regimes are one-party states, characteristically dominated by a highly centralised Communist Party. Further, through what in Marxist ideology is called the party's 'leading role', control is exercised by the regime effectively over the whole of the society. Consequently, 'institutions which in the West are more or less independent of the political system, including the press, the trade unions and the courts, are under the direct control of the party leadership.'[7]

On the basis of such strict criteria the number of unambiguously accepted and firmly established communist regimes is not only effectively limited in numbers, but is also mainly centred in the industrialised North rather than in the economically under-developed South of the globe – though there are important exceptions: China, Cuba, Kampuchea, North Korea, Laos and

Vietnam. From this perspective therefore those growing numbers of southern states which identify with communism and which, collectively, have been described as forming 'The New Communist Third World',[8] are viewed as currently exhibiting patterns of politics more characteristic of their Third World counterparts than of the well-established Marxist regimes which form the core of the Second World pattern.

Third World regimes. However, the very ideological variability among Third World states – some identifying themselves with and practising forms of liberal-democracy and others emulating and practising Marxism – underlines the difficulty of describing and classifying the large number of the world's states which remain unaccounted for after the First and Second World patterns have been described. Nevertheless, despite their political and economic heterogeneity, it remains of some use to view the states of the Third World as a political as well as an economic entity.

For a start these states, with a few exceptions (e.g. Afghanistan, Ethiopia, Iran, Liberia, Thailand and Turkey), were a product of the end of the European colonial empires, which resulted in the independence of the Latin American states in the nineteenth century and those of Asia and Africa in the twentieth. Consequently, these states may be seen as essentially artificial creations, with their geographical boundaries defined during the processes of colonisation and decolonisation in an often random or capricious manner and with their organisational cores made up of alien rather than indigenous institutions.

The result is a characteristic lack of any inherited sense of national unity and identity, particularly noticeable in the newest states of Asia and Africa which achieved their independence only in the years after the Second World War. These are states created before corresponding nations existed – state-nations rather than conventional nation-states – in which loyalties often remain tied to the narrower divisions of tribe or region, and where wider loyalties to nation and state are emerging only slowly, if at all. Consequently the governments of such states are often accorded little legitimacy by their populations and suffer from an acute lack of public support. Politics is practised in an atmosphere of permanent distrust, suspicion and fear that what one group receives must either be taken from or threaten all other groups in the state. Formal rules of the political arena are non-existent or ignored. Winners take all, and losers simply wait and plot for the first opportunity to remove them by whatever means, legal or frequently illegal.[9]

Furthermore, these Third World states are, with a few exceptions, poor – some of them desperately so. Seventy per cent of the world's peoples live in these states, but collectively they contribute no more than twelve per cent of the world's production. Indeed it is on the basis of economic indicators and performance that the boundaries of the Third World are habitually defined. The Development Assistance Committee of the OECD (Organisation for Economic Co-operation and Development – the principal economic organisation of the industrialised Northern states) provides one of the most widely accepted lists of 'developing countries'. This covers all states in Africa except South Africa, all in America except Canada and the USA, all in Asia apart from Japan, all in Oceania with the exception of Australia and New Zealand, and also (more problematically) covers certain of the poorer European states (Cyprus, Gibraltar, Greece, Malta, Portugal, Spain, Turkey and Yugoslavia). The rest of the world's states are defined as economically developed. More recently, in 1980, the international Brandt Commission published a largely similar list of one hundred Southern states (a term now used synonymously with Third World) but which departed from the OECD's list by including South Africa and excluding all European states except Turkey.

However, within this large grouping of LDCs (Less Developed Countries) there exist wide disparities of wealth and economic potential, notably between the generally very poor states of Africa and Asia and the economically more advanced states of Latin America. Moreover, when the economic achievements and potential of individual Third World states are considered, the contrasts become even more marked. On the one hand, there are the oil-rich OPEC (Organisation of Petroleum Exporting Countries) states such as Kuwait with its average income per head of $15,000, the world's highest, as well as the seven so-called NICs (Newly Industrialising Countries) of East Asia, South-East Asia and Latin America. These latter states have sustained high rates of economic growth and have expanded their manufacturing output and exports rapidly – Argentina, Brazil, Hong Kong, Korea, Mexico, Singapore, and Taiwan are all examples of this category. On the other hand, there are the often heavily over-populated states of what the Brandt Commission defined as the globe's two 'poverty belts'. These stretch right across the middle of the African continent and extend from the Persian Gulf across south Asia into eastern Asia respectively. Most of the 31 Least Developed Countries (LLDCs) of the world, (countries with average per capita incomes of less than $200) are to be found in these poverty belts (21 in Africa, nine in Asia, one in the Pacific and one in the Caribbean). However, the collective population of these states is only approximately 270 million. Since the World Bank has estimated that 800 million people (almost 40 per cent of the South's population) are living in utter destitution without sufficient income to secure the basic necessities for survival, the problem of acute poverty is one which affects most Third World states. Indeed roughly sixty or seventy of these countries form what has sometimes been described as a Fourth World of 'have-nots'.

Moreover, similar (if by no means identical) social, political and economic backgrounds have led to similar *internal* political predicaments and responses. If just one aspect of Third World government had to be singled out as typical it would have to be chronic instability, with regimes changing rapidly and often chaotically between civilian and military rulers, as well as between competing factions within these two elite groups. However, whilst on the surface such states may appear to be in constant turmoil, this picture is misleading, for the successive governments and regimes frequently lack the power to secure their own survival, let alone make fundamental changes in policy. Politics and government in these states encourages seamanship rather than navigation, and has been defined as more a matter of 'staying afloat rather than going somewhere.'[10]

Inevitably, in such states, successive regimes whether civilian or military, rule in a predominantly authoritarian and often overtly coercive manner. Rulers, whether civilian or military, concerned mainly with their own personal and political survival, tend to show an excessive concern for stability and order. In their defence of the interests of the privileged governing few against the demands of the excluded many, repression frequently becomes the easiest option. In a summary which is based on the specific conditions pertaining in Africa but which has a much wider relevance to Third World regimes generally, Professor Dennis Austin has captured the essence of this type of authoritarian rule where, generally speaking:

> instruments of *control* – the civil service, police and armed forces – have been strengthened and expanded; those with any degree of *autonomy* – universities, the newspapers, the courts, and the constitution – have been curbed; and those of a *representative* nature – parliaments, trade unions, local councils – have been minimised or put into recess.[11]

Conclusion

At this point, however, it must be emphasised once again that it is impossible to fit every contemporary state unambiguously into only one of these three categories. In particular the boundary between the Second and Third World patterns has, in recent years, become blurred, with an increasingly large number of Third World states specifically identifying themselves (with varying degrees of commitment in reality) as non-competitive communist regimes. Similarly, other Third World states, such as Costa Rica and India, have over recent decades (as well as a number of other Third World states over shorter periods of time) sustained political competition and stability of a type and to an extent comparable to their First World counterparts, thereby highlighting the flexibility of the boundary between First and Third World patterns. Nonetheless, the present division between First and Second World patterns appears to be clear, unambiguous and absolute. 'There are no centrally planned countries with pluralist democratic politics, even though many democratic socialists have aspired for more than a hundred years to establish such a combination and hope yet to succeed.'[12] Interestingly, this proposition does not operate in reverse. Whilst the political democracies have competitive market-based economies, by no means all the states with such economies are democratic.

Consequently, it becomes logical to view this division of contemporary states into three distinguishable worlds of political development as a continuum, rather than as a series of clear divides. From this perspective the Third World states stand, as it were, between the states of the other two Worlds, with a number of them consciously seeking to emulate and, in some cases, successfully adopting some or many of the political characteristics and practices of their more economically and politically developed counterparts. Yet, despite these overlaps, the great bulk of Third World states have more in common with each other politically than they do with states of either of the other two political patterns.

The chapters which follow will provide the raw material on the basis of which this simple threefold regime classification can be expanded and refined. This task will specifically be undertaken in the concluding chapter when the differentiating characteristics of the three different types of regimes will be examined once again. However, comparisons and contrasts between these three different types of regime are to be found throughout the book. In the case of the First and Second World patterns the analysis will frequently concentrate on single 'representative' (if not always typical) states, the USA and the USSR respectively, whilst in the case of the Third World pattern the analysis will be less specific, seeking to summarise experiences common to many of these states.

2 Political Leadership: Executives in the Modern World

Traditional classifications of governmental leadership

Regimes have frequently been classified by their most 'visible' features, which, in many cases, has meant a classification based on either the different forms or the different styles that political leadership has taken. Thus, until relatively recently, constitutions were frequently divided into monarchical and republican forms, with this division also viewed as corresponding to the difference between absolute, autocratic and dictatorial systems on the one hand, and limited, popular, and democratic governments on the other. However, just as from a broad historical perspective most regimes have been monarchical – in the sense that they were ruled by hereditary leaders claiming either divine or traditional rights to govern – so in the contemporary world such traditional forms of leadership have all but disappeared, with their last remaining examples to be found mainly in the Middle East. Consequently a division between republican and monarchical forms of government is, in today's circumstances, more or less meaningless. Many of the surviving monarchies, such as the British, Dutch and Swedish examples, exist within what would traditionally have been described as limited, popular and democratic regimes. Many of the world's republics, on the other hand, which form the bulk of contemporary regimes, could be termed autocratic or dictatorial in the very traditional sense that they possess absolute rather than limited forms of government.

An equally traditional constitutional classification, but one with much greater contemporary relevance, is that which divides parliamentary from presidential executives. Originally this classification was designed to correspond to what was viewed as the more fundamental division between those constitutions which embodied the idea of a clear separation of 'powers' or functions between three branches of government, executive, legislative and judicial (presidential), and those which did not adopt this division of functions (parliamentary). The relevance of this classification has not disappeared, despite a general acceptance that the theory of the separation of powers on which it was based has little or no empirical relevance today. It is sometimes argued that there are three basic powers or functions of government – making laws (legislative), putting these laws into effect (executive) and interpreting the law by settling the resultant disputes (judicial). However, these separate functions are not the sole property of one corresponding institution of government. On the contrary, all governmental institutions tend to carry out a variety of these functions. In short, all governmental structures are multifunctional, with each institution or branch of government characteristically carrying out several aspects of all three of the tasks or functions of government.

Nevertheless, the three basic institutions or branches of government do exist and, as we have seen, this separate existence is acknowledged and enshrined in contemporary constitutions. Why, then, does this threefold division occur? The answer is historical, stemming from developments which took place in Europe, the cradle of the modern nation-state, from the sixteenth century onwards. Until this early modern period, governmental power tended to be undivided, in Europe as in the rest of the world, in the sense that rulers allowed no institutional rivals to their absolute power. The state was 'a monolith'.[1] However, as a result of communication and commercial and industrial developments, new centres of social and economic power emerged within the state, and these groups naturally sought a commensurate share of political power. Clearly, this aim involved a division of the formerly monolithic power of the ruler, and the method used to effect this division was either to take over existing governmental institutions or to create new institutions. These institutions were assemblies or parliaments, and courts. The former claimed to represent the views of the ruled, and eventually they won rights over the raising of finance and the making of laws. The latter claimed their independent right to interpret these laws; laws which were held to be equally binding both on ruler and ruled. These take-over bids were buttressed by claims that separate executive, legislative and judicial institutions would promote freedom and justice. 'The successful enforcing of these claims, where it occurred, transformed the state from a monolith into a trialith. It is with such trialiths that most of us in the West are still living'[2] – and, indeed, in the East and the South.

Thus, historically, executives formed the central core or kernel of governments, out of which, from the sixteenth century, separate legislative and judicial institutions progressively emerged and broke off. As a result, executive branches of government are more diverse in both their functions and their structures than the other two branches. 'Legislatures and judiciaries are, so to speak, firms that specialise,' suggests Professor King. 'Executives are conglomerates.'[3] In particular, the executive branch of government contains both politicians and civil servants and consists of both political and bureaucratic institutions. Frequently therefore, in academic literature, the term 'executive' is used to refer to both politicians and civil servants, but invariably in this literature it will refer only to 'top management', that is decision-making politicians and very senior civil servants. However, there is much less agreement about the precise composition of this 'top management'. Consequently the term 'executive' may refer to what in Britain is usually termed 'the government' and in the USA 'the administration'. Or it may refer to an even narrower set of ruling institutions and individuals who possess ultimate decision-making power, such as the Politburo and General Secretary in the USSR and other communist states, the ruling juntas in military regimes, and, of course, presidents, prime ministers and their cabinets.

The term 'executive' will be used here in both these senses, seeking to encompass all major political decision-makers, or better still the formulators of important policy decisions – whether politicians or bureaucrats, civilian or military. It therefore encompasses all those individuals or institutions whose responsibility it is to undertake the primary historical function of the executive, providing political leadership. Thus, both senior politicians and senior bureaucrats are incorporated into the definition of the executive. The rationale for this is that the border between the *political* executive (the government) and the *bureaucratic* executive (the administration) does not correspond to any clear difference in their activities. In the modern state it is impossible to claim that governments alone make policy, and that administrations simply implement it. Rather, policy-making involves a partnership between government and administration. Nevertheless, even if there exists an overlap of functions between government and administration, they are, generally, well separated in terms of their personnel. The two groups characteristically pursue quite separate careers, with bureaucrats habitually making a career of administration. This professionalism contrasts with the comparative 'amateurism' of politicians, who have been described as being 'catapulted from outside over the heads of administrators,' theoretically at least, to lead the bureaucracy.[4] Moreover, governments also tend to be distinguished from bureaucracies in the manner in which they operate, with the former taking the limelight and the latter operating in the shadows. Consequently, this chapter will cover mainly the political executive or government. The bureaucratic executive or the administration is left aside to be analysed in Chapter 7 (civilian bureaucrats) and Chapter 8 (the military or 'armed bureaucrats'), except when, as in military governments, bureaucrats occupy the institutions of the political executive and thereby force themselves into this chapter.

Heads of government: types of chief executive
A classification of contemporary types of political executives may most logically begin by focusing on heads of governments. In particular this focus on 'chief executives', that is, those in charge of the 'overall aspects of policy making,' neatly underlines, as Professor Blondel points out, the 'varied and diverse' nature of executive types among contemporary regimes.[5] Nevertheless these wide variations and diversities are hardly obvious when the titles of these leaders are considered, since most still fall under the three historically dominant categories – monarchs, presidents and prime ministers. However, the precise name used varies, particularly in the case of monarchs, a category which incorporates kings, emperors, grand-dukes and emirs. Similarly prime ministers may be called 'Chairman of the Council of Ministers' (communist states) or 'Chancellor' (as in Austria and Germany).

VERNON REGIONAL
JUNIOR COLLEGE LIBRARY

Monarchs. The number of ruling (as opposed to simply reigning) monarchs has steadily declined since the Second World War, and this decline is likely to continue, despite the restoration of the Spanish monarchy during the 1970s. Traditional, ruling, monarchs are today an isolated governmental form confined to a few states in the Near and Middle East and the Himalayas, and to Swaziland in Africa. As Professor Blondel comments 'this system of government is obviously only a relic of the past,'[6] and its survival today and into the future depends on either oil wealth or isolation from external influences.

Presidents. Since most contemporary states are republics, and since republics are normally led by presidents, it is not surprising to find that the largest group of contemporary heads of government are presidents. Nor is it surprising to find that this one title covers a wide variety of very different forms of rule. About fifty contemporary regimes are presidential, and they are mainly to be found in Latin America and Africa. The routes towards presidentialism in the two regions differed. The example of the USA influenced the development of a constitutionally restricted presidential system in nineteenth-century Latin America. Africa, on the other hand, used the strong presidential rule of General de Gaulle in France as its main institutional model. In both regions, however, the presidency has tended to become a vehicle for highly personalised systems of rule. Both regions today are charcterised by chronic political instability with civilian and military governments alternating in cyclical patterns. This alternation is particularly noticeable in Latin America where the pattern can be observed over a period of a century or more. As a result, the presidency in Latin America is commonly referred to not only as the highest civilian office, but also as the highest military rank!

Consequently, at least as it is practised in the great majority of states in which it has been adopted, presidentialism can be viewed as the modern counterpart to, and successor of the now declining absolute monarchies. Its appeal in Third World regions, to both civilian and military rulers, perhaps lies mainly in its apparent simplicity. In particular, presidentialism can concentrate power (theoretically at least) in the hands of one individual, who is responsible to no other political institutions, but only, if at all,

VERNON REGIONAL
JUNIOR COLLEGE LIBRARY

to 'the people'. It thereby avoids the necessity, inherent in the operation of parliamentary and prime ministerial systems, either for the complexities of a party system or for the negotiation of an intricate balance of power between competing leaders or institutions of government. Many Third World political leaders, including many civilian leaders, have felt that the complexities and delays involved in the need for constant communication between prime minister, cabinet, party and legislature, outweighed any advantages that this form of government might bring, preferring the certainty and ease of executive predominance promised by a presidential system.

Certainly the apparent simplicity of presidential rule accounts for the system's overwhelming popularity among military leaders. Such leaders are prone to claim that their right to govern stems directly from the people and to deny the necessity for the existence of any other intermediary institutions in the form of parties, parliaments, or even in many cases elections. As General Mobutu modestly told his troops following a successful military coup in the Central African state of Zaire in 1965, 'I am President of the Republic for five years.' And so he remains to this day. In many cases, however, the adoption of highly personalised forms of presidentialism has inevitably reinforced the characteristic instability of African and Latin American regimes. In these states, particularly in the absence of effective political parties, no institutionalised methods exist, short of a forcible change of president and regime, for bringing effective political pressures to bear on the leader. Significantly, in the comparatively unusual example of the Latin American state of Mexico, where a powerful presidency is counterbalanced by a relatively powerful political party, the outcome has been, in Third World terms, an impressive level of political stability. This stability is achieved through a convention that each president retires after a single six-year term. Mexico, it is said, avoids dictatorship only by changing its dictator every six years! The other side of the coin can be illustrated by the experience of the Central African Republic, whose military leader Jean-Badel Bokassa, a fervent admirer of Napoleon, aspired to imperial status, and in 1977, had himself so crowned, and his state re-designated as the Central African Empire. Equally significantly, his reign lasted only until 1979, when he was removed by a military coup d'état.

At the other end of the spectrum of presidential power (and at the other end of the spectrum of political stability), lies the constitutionally limited and politically constrained American presidency. Despite its separate election and formal independence from all other political institutions, the American presidency operates in a system of complicated inter-institutional competition. The explanation for the existence of this system lies in the cynical view of human nature held by the 'founding fathers' of the American constitution. As James Madison argued, it was a 'reflection on human nature, that . . . devices should be necessary to control the abuses of government.' As a result he stressed that it was imperative to oblige the government 'to control itself . . . Ambition must be made to counteract ambition.'[7] Hence, the doctrine of the separation of powers was married to the idea of 'checks and balances'. This latter principle involves the partial sharing of powers between the different institutions of government whilst their personnel are kept strictly separate (see Figure 2.1). The outcome has aptly been described as a system of 'separated institutions *sharing* powers',[8] and its impact on the presidency has been to constrain the powers of the office in a way which makes the American system 'a very special case' among presidencies. Indeed, suggests Professor Blondel, 'if a strict definition of limited presidential rule were to be adopted, only the United States would consistently fit the model and only Costa Rica, Venezuela and perhaps Colombia would fit it fairly consistently during the postwar period'[9] – *fairly* consistently, since whilst all three Latin American states are currently under civilian rule, the last two have suffered periods of military rule since the Second World War. Certainly, none of the other contemporary presidential systems could be considered as examples of American-style limited presidential regimes.

Prime ministers. Historically, prime ministers, the third major type of chief executive, emerged from beneath the wings of presidents or monarchs, entrusted originally by the latter with the subordinate tasks of leading the state bureaucracy and co-ordinating the institutions of governmental decision-making. As a result their effective powers vary markedly in the thirty or so

Figure 2.1   *'Ambition must be made to counteract ambition': the separation of powers and checks and balances in the USA*

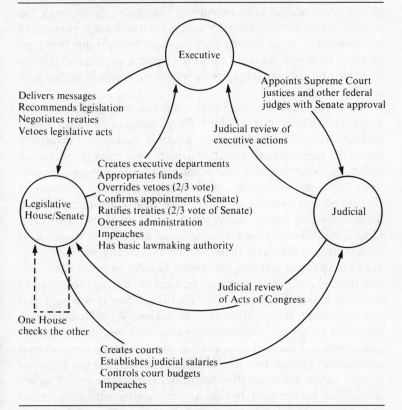

Executive

Delivers messages
Recommends legislation
Negotiates treaties
Vetoes legislative acts

Appoints Supreme Court
justices and other federal
judges with Senate approval

Judicial review of
executive actions

Creates executive departments
Appropriates funds
Overrides vetoes (2/3 vote)
Confirms appointments (Senate)
Ratifies treaties (2/3 vote of Senate)
Oversees administration
Impeaches
Has basic lawmaking authority

Legislative
House/Senate

Judicial

Judicial review
of Acts of Congress

One House
checks the other

Creates courts
Establishes judicial salaries
Controls court budgets
Impeaches

Source: William J Keefe *et al.*, *American Democracy: Institutions, Politics, and Policies*, Homewood, Illinois, The Dorsey Press, 1983, Figure 1:1, p.30

states which practise prime ministerial government, half of them monarchical in form and half republican. Significantly, like presidential government, prime ministerial regimes are regionally concentrated, occurring mainly in the Western First World states, where three-quarters of all regimes are parliamentary in form. Additionally, parliamentary regimes have spread via colonisation and decolonisation to the states of South and South-East Asia and

Australasia. Outside these areas prime ministerial government, although invariably instituted in British colonies as a precondition of independence (as most recently in the case of Zimbabwe), has tended not to survive for very long after the formal granting of independence; it has usually been replaced by a presidential form of rule. However, isolated pockets of prime ministerial government do still survive among the anglophone states of both Africa and the Caribbean.

The explanation for this relative unpopularity of prime ministerial government in the Third World appears to lie in its inherently collective rather than personal emphasis. Invariably based on some variation of the British style cabinet system, in which, in theory at least, the prime minister is only *primus inter pares* (first among equals), it therefore entails the problem of sharing powers between ministers. The clearly hierarchical presidential systems more easily avoid these problems. However, some Third World prime ministers are able, by sheer force of personality, to dominate their cabinets in a clearly presidential or even monarchical fashion. Mrs Indira Gandhi in India was often, and rightly, cited as an example, particularly during the period of declared national emergency, 1975–1977, when it was said that 'Indira became India.' However, most Third World leaders have preferred to secure and institutionalise their personal predominance within a formally presidential system. Moreover, whilst a presidential system does not necessarily presuppose the existence of any other representative institutions, the essence of prime ministerial government lies in its relationship with parliaments and parties. In all prime ministerial regimes, the cabinet or its equivalent is closely associated with the legislature, usually, as in Britain, with ministers drawn from the parliament and responsible to it for the conduct of the government. The achievement of governmental stability in this type of regime requires that the executive maintains the continued support of the legislature. This support can only be guaranteed through the operation of a disciplined political party controlling a majority of parliamentary seats and votes.

Other forms of executive leadership. Although most contemporary regimes can be defined in the traditional manner as possessing either monarchical, presidential or prime ministerial (parliamentary) executives, these three categories certainly do not exhaust the variety of executive types in contemporary regimes. First, there are two further major types of executive leadership, one taking the form of ruling collectivities or councils and the other the ruling party leaders (first or general secretaries) in communist regimes. Second, the increasing number of dual, shared, or hybrid forms of executive must be acknowledged.

Ruling collectivities or councils tend to be commonest in military regimes where the designation of one officer as chief executive frequently obscures the genuinely shared character of the executive leadership group which takes power following a *coup d'état*. Although these groups adopt a variety of different, and sometimes exotic, names, such as National Liberation Council and National Redemption Council (two examples taken from the West African state of Ghana), they tend collectively and in general, to be referred to as *juntas*. Typically these military juntas, while remaining dominated by military officers, also incorporate some civilian members into the ruling group. The powers of these bodies vary widely. Some exhibit the genuinely collective exercise of authority and leadership. Others are closer to the type of one-man presidential dictatorship practised by Idi Amin in Uganda between 1971 and 1979 where the Council of Ministers remained a rubber stamp. Curiously only one civilian regime currently possesses this form of collective chief executive – Switzerland, with its Federal Council, among whose seven members the presidency rotates annually. In Latin America, however, Uruguay adopted a conciliar form of regime between 1952 and 1967.

First or general secretaries of ruling Communist parties, the final type of contemporary political leader, form a homogeneous group who have emerged as effective chief executives, but not always as titular heads of state. For the latter purpose the office of president exists in communist regimes. In the USSR the presidency, which involves performing ceremonial functions and receiving ambassadors, is held by the chairman of the Presidium (or standing body) of the Soviet legislature – the Supreme Soviet – which will be covered in full in Chapter 3. Interestingly, this office was held concurrently from 1977 to 1985, by the party

Figure 2.2 Executive leadership in the USSR

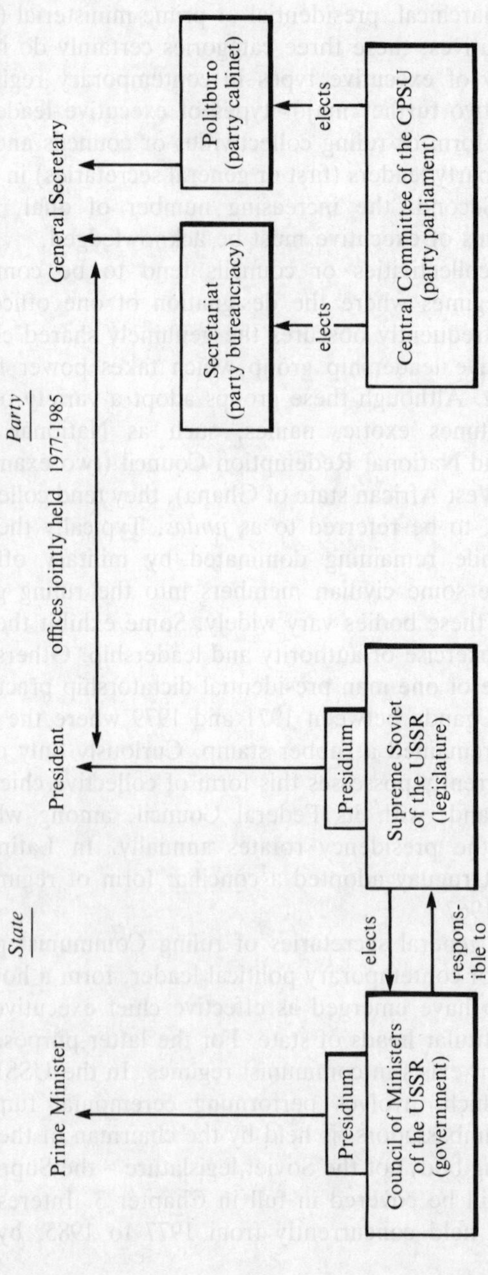

Party (offices jointly held 1977–1985)

- Central Committee of the CPSU (party parliament) elects Politburo (party cabinet)
- Central Committee of the CPSU elects General Secretary
- Central Committee of the CPSU elects Secretariat (party bureaucracy)

State

- Supreme Soviet of the USSR (legislature) elects Presidium → President
- Supreme Soviet of the USSR (legislature) elects Council of Ministers of the USSR (government); Council of Ministers responsible to Supreme Soviet
- Council of Ministers of the USSR (government) — Presidium → Prime Minister

leader. However, in most Second World states, other than the USSR and Czechoslovakia, which also has an individual presidency, the Presidium (sometimes, as in East Germany, called 'State Council') of the state legislature functions as a collective presidency. In all these states of the Second World the ruling party is increasingly formally and openly recognised as the most important policy-making institution. It possesses its own specialised institutions which parallel those of the formal (constitutionally recognised) legislative and executive institutions of government – the latter being collectively referred to as 'the state'. In particular the party's Politburo (chaired by the party leader) forms the system's equivalent of a cabinet, and the party's Central Committee is frequently referred to as a second, and more important, parliament. Similarly the party Secretariat (also chaired by the party leader) has, as one of its many executive functions, the duty to oversee and supervise the 'state' bureaucracy which is formally headed by a prime minister. This form (see Figure 2.2) of dual and duplicating party/state systems of governmental institutions is unique to the regimes of the Second World, and results in a novel type of political leadership found in no other regimes. It therefore remains, like the four other major executive forms, relatively concentrated geographically.

Executive dualism: trends towards shared leadership. It might be anticipated that with the complexities of government increasing in line with the rapidly expanding ambitions and responsibilities of contemporary regimes, that there would almost inevitably be a tendency towards the emergence of new hybrid forms of 'dual' or 'shared' executive leadership. These developments evolved simply as a recognition that the burdens of governmental decision-making are such as to require the development of more effective specialisation and division of labour within executives. In some regimes, of which the USA provides an excellent, if unusually generous, example, the acknowledgement of the fact that 'the President needs help'[10] has taken the form of 'institutionalizing' the presidency by providing the individual office-holder with a personal staff of hundreds (the White House Office) and a supporting bureaucracy of thousands (the Executive Office of the President). In other regimes this recognition of the increasing decisional burdens placed on chief executives has been accompanied by the adoption of a new division of functions and responsibilities within the executive.

Restricted before the twentieth century mainly to the division between monarch and prime minister, executive dualism now commonly divides power between prime ministers and presidents, and prime ministers and Communist party leaders. Characteristically, in all cases, this division of responsibilities gives the prime minister responsibility for supervision for administration and bureaucracy. This type of 'dual' leadership is particularly common among the regimes of the communist Second World as well as in the Middle East (where it occurs in both monarchical and presidential regimes), but it has spread, albeit more thinly, to all other parts of the globe, appearing, according to Professor Blondel, in 48 states in 1976. The most typical pattern (for example characteristic of all the communist states, as well as a number of non-communist ones), is for a system of unequal power-sharing to exist, with the prime minister in a subordinate position. France, for instance, has, since the inauguration of the Fifth Republic in 1958, had what originally appeared to be a two-headed executive. However, a combination of institutional developments (particularly the establishment of a system of direct election for the presidency in 1962), and an acceptance by successive prime ministers of their subordinate status, has led to a predominant presidency. Given its advantages in terms of a division of executive labour it is perhaps unsurprising that recently inaugurated constitutions, like that of France, have often tended to incorporate such hybrid (i.e. neither purely parliamentary nor purely presidential) forms. Indeed this trend towards shared or dual executive leadership is the most marked of the rather limited changes in the global pattern of executive leadership which have occurred since 1945, as a glance at Table 2.1 will underline.

Similarly, given the highly unstable political conditions in many Third World states, the attractions of such 'hybrid' forms of chief executive have become ever more obvious to states which are seeking to combine the advantages of the (potential) executive stability and continuity provided by a directly elected presidency with the advantages inherent in parliamentary-style control over legislative institutions. Thus, the type of presidentialism increas-

Table 2.1   Types of chief executive

	1945 or at independence	1976
Single		
Monarchies	8	6
Presidential	51	51
Prime ministerial	40	32
Shared		
Monarch and prime minister	14	8
President and prime minister	15	23
Party secretary and prime minister	9	17
Councils of equals	1	1

Source: Adapted from Jean Blondel, *World Leaders* (Sage, 1982), Table 2, p. 53, and Table 4, p. 55

ingly sought by Third World states tends to be much closer to that of France than that of the USA, with the president dominating the whole political landscape. In these states the presidency directly controls (often with the assistance of a prime minister) not only the rest of the political executive but also, through disciplined political parties, the legislature too.

Contemporary governments: two examples

The USSR and the USA therefore provide usefully contrasting examples of contemporary governmental structures, as well as examples of two very different types of answer to the question of how to attempt to maintain political control over burgeoning governmental institutions.

Party-state partnership in the USSR. One of the most important features of the Soviet system of government is that it eliminates, to a large extent, the conventional Western distinction between politician and bureaucrat. On the one hand this system provides an institutional structure of government which seeks to divide policy-making from administration by placing them in the hands of different governmental institutions. On the other hand it also seeks to keep the latter subservient through the activities of the Communist party.

In the Soviet Union, the Council of Ministers is described in the 1977 Constitution (Article 128) as 'the Government of the USSR' and as 'the highest executive and administrative body.' However, in practice, like all 'state' organs, it is subordinated to the two leading decision-making institutions of the Communist party, the Politburo and the Secretariat. The Council of Ministers may most sensibly be viewed therefore as performing functions of an administrative and managerial nature. Its members have achieved their position through pursuing careers in the Soviet bureaucracy, moving up the civil service hierarchy within the ministries which the Council controls and manages. At the same time all important posts within the Soviet bureaucracy are subject to direct Communist party control through a system known as the *nomenklatura* (which will be described in detail in Chapters 5 and 7). Whilst not all Soviet bureaucrats are Communist party members, all occupants of the highest posts, such as members of the Council of Ministers, will inevitably not only be members but will also be senior party functionaries. Many of them will also be members of the party's own parliament, the Central Committee of the Communist party. Although, since the downfall of Nikita Khrushchev in 1964, the leadership of the party and the chairmanship of the Council of Ministers have been in separate hands, the prime minister has also, invariably, been a member of the party's own 'cabinet', the Politburo. Thus, an overlap of memberships extending to the highest institutions of state and party reinforces party control of promotions in underlining and securing, in theory at least, the party's leading role and guiding function in the Soviet political system.

Due to the fact that in Second World states the government is responsible for all facets of industrial, agricultural, commercial, educational and artistic life, the Councils of Ministers in Communist states generally are very large bodies. The Soviet insistence on having a separate ministry for each separate industry ensures that the Council of Ministers of the USSR is particularly large. Its membership of over 100 (132 in 1985) makes it far too large a body for decision-making, and, in practice, the full Council of Ministers of the USSR meets only briefly approximately once a month. However, its chairman, the prime minister, and a small group of senior ministers from the Presidium of the Council of Ministers, form a kind of inner cabinet in which the real decisions on administrative policy are made. In April 1984 this 'inner cabinet' had a membership of fourteen. The Soviet constitution states that the Presidium shall function as a standing body of the Council of Ministers, and, meeting weekly or even more often, it is empowered to deal with questions relating to guidance of the economy and related matters of general state administration concerning, for example, education, health and welfare.

Its most important functions are to ensure that the national budget and the national industrial plans are prepared, co-ordinated and executed. It performs these tasks, however, as the agent of the party's policy-making institutions, Politburo and Secretariat. Accordingly, the membership of the Council of Ministers, and particularly its Presidium is closely interlocked with the top party leadership, both in the party's Central Committee and in its Politburo. About one-third of the membership of the latter tends to be held by state 'government' leaders, whilst all members of the Council of Ministers tend to have seats on the Central Committee and generally comprise about 20 per cent of its total membership.

The Politburo and Secretariat, and the State Council of Ministers and its Presidium are the most significant decision-making institutions within the highly complex form of governmental organisation evolved by Second World states. However, two further institutions must also be mentioned in this context – the legislature and its controlling Presidium. For the constitutional importance, if not the real impact, of the legislature and its Presidium in such states goes far beyond the titular and ceremonial functions associated with the presidency. As the Soviet constitution claims, it is the legislature which appoints the membership of the Council of Ministers (Article 129) and the latter is held to be 'responsible and accountable' to the former and is obliged to make regular reports on its work (Article 130). Moreover public calls have been made by recent Soviet party and legislative leaders for the legislature to exert a genuine authority over the 'state' government and its subordinate bureaucracy, and increasingly to control, in a meaningful way, the activities of the Council of Ministers and its subordinate ministries. In practice, however, the state legislature in the USSR, as in all other Second World states except, possibly, Yugoslavia, retains an influence over the state executive which is more symbolic than real. Nevertheless, despite the merely formal and symbolic nature of the subordination of the Council of Ministers outside Yugoslavia, a glance at Figure 2.3 below will show that no overlap of membership exists between the Presidium of the Supreme Soviet of the USSR and the Council of Ministers. This upholds a Soviet governmental convention forbidding overlapping membership between two institutions, where one is formally responsible to the other. With this one exception the overlap of personnel between leading party and state institutions is very extensive.

Thus, Second World governments are 'dual' in the sense that they divide the governmental functions between separate party and state institutions. Yet they are, on further examination, rather more complicated than that description suggests, since they further divide governmental responsibilities between different institutions within the two specialised structures of 'party'

Figure 2.3   Interlocking membership between state and party institutions in the USSR

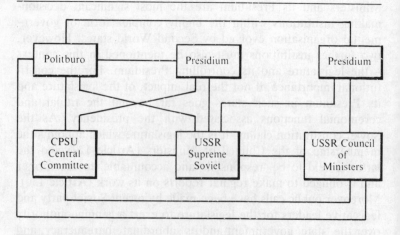

Source: Ronald J Hill & Peter Frank, *The Soviet Communist Party* (Allen and Unwin, 2nd ed, 1983), Figure 5.1, p.116.

and 'state' respectively. It is therefore quite unrealistic to refer, in any but the most formal of senses, to *the* Soviet government, since the functions of governmental decision-making and adminstrative supervision are undertaken by at least five separate institutions. Second World states therefore possess governmental structures markedly more institutionally divided than the comparatively simple united structures to be found in British-style cabinet governments.

Extreme governmental decentralisation and division: the USA
However, it is in the USA that governmental division and decentralisation occurs in its most extreme form, since America lacks even the political cement of a strong party system to counteract the impact of divided institutions. Paradoxically, at first sight, the American presidential system appears thoroughly hierarchical. Thus, the chief executive is increasingly able to organise and reorganise the executive 'branch' of government, and is also able to appoint his governmental subordinates, not only in the Cabinet, but also in his own large personal advisory bureaucracy, as well as up to 2,000 senior civil servants (albeit with the agreement of one house of the legislature, the Senate). Yet the practice of American government today only rarely (except in the field of foreign policy) seems 'presidential' in the clear hierarchical sense that may justifiably be used to describe Third World examples of the system. In particular, the peculiarly decentralised and undisciplined nature of the American party system, combined with the deliberately designed system of institutional competition between executive and legislature, ensures that government in the USA lacks both unity and, frequently, direction compared to other states in both First and Second Worlds. Commentators, following Richard Neustadt's pioneering study, *Presidential Power*, have consistently pointed out that the American president's power is the power to 'persuade' other institutions and individuals to do what he wishes, and that his function is less one of directing and ordering others than of influencing or inducing them to behave in desired ways.[11] Similarly, the American government, even more than those of Second World states, has increasingly become divided into a number of more or less independent political units, which the president, despite his own enormous personal staff, has

grave difficulty in co-ordinating, let alone leading. In short, American government, more than that of any other contemporary regime, can truly be said to have become 'a government of strangers'[12] – too large and too diverse to be controlled by one man, or perhaps to be controlled at all.

These developments have occurred relatively recently, stemming from the rapid growth in the size and scope of the Federal administration and government during the presidencies of F. D. Roosevelt from 1933 to 1945, when the economic and social crisis of the Great Depression was swiftly followed by the even greater national crisis occasioned by the Second World War. What occurred then, and has continued to occur since, has meant that American government has grown remarkably both in terms of personnel and of institutions. First the New Deal and then the Second World War proliferated federal government agencies. Subsequently, post-war federal initiatives in the fields of civil rights, housing, transport and urban affairs were reinforced by the concerns of the 1970s, in the form of governmental involvement in the areas of consumer protection, and energy and environmental conservation. All these developments were duly institutionalised by the establishment of federal governmental organisations. Indeed, the proliferation of departments and agencies has increasingly frustrated attempts by the president and his assistants to maintain hierarchical control over a mushrooming federal bureaucracy, while the American 'government' has come to seem more like a number of independent and frequently competing agencies, rather than a single entity. As a result, the executive branch has been described as a 'monster' whose 75 or so component institutions 'are arranged with clarity only on paper'[13] (see Figure 2.4).

First, there is the president's cabinet, which is composed of the thirteen secretaries of state – who head the executive departments of state which form the core of the federal governmental administration – plus any other members the president chooses to nominate. In these departments of state the president appoints, with the Senate's confirmation, not only the Secretary who heads the department, but under-secretaries, deputy under-secretaries and assistant secretaries of state. Conventionally, however, the president is granted a virtually free hand in these

Figure 2.4   US Federal Government: executive branch (main institutions)

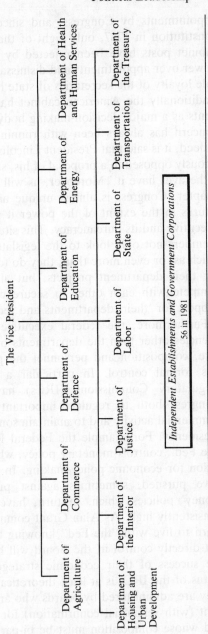

The President

Executive Office of the President

White House Office
Office of Management and Budget
Council of Economic Advisers
National Security Council
Office of Policy Development
Office of the US Trade Representative

Council on Environmental Quality
Office of Science and Technology Policy
Office of Administration

The Vice President

Department of Agriculture
Department of Housing and Urban Development
Department of the Interior
Department of Commerce
Department of Justice
Department of Labor
Department of Defence
Department of Education
Department of State
Department of Energy
Department of Transportation
Department of Health and Human Services
Department of the Treasury

Independent Establishments and Government Corporations
56 in 1981

Source: William J Keefe, *et al.*, eds, *American Democracy: Institutions, Politics, and Policies* (Illinois, The Dorsey Press, 1983), Figure 11.3, p. 352.

appointments by Congress, and since the inauguration of the constitution in 1787, only eight of the president's nominees for cabinet posts have been rejected by the Senate. Nevertheless, power over appointment (and dismissal) does not ensure that the sole loyalty of the secretaries of state lies with the president. For traditionally the American cabinet has not been used by presidents as a major decision-making body and the secretaries' main concern has always been with running their own departments. Indeed, it is said that President Lincoln, finding the cabinet unanimously opposed to a proposal of his, stated 'Seven noes, one aye – the ayes have it.' Moreover, as will be underlined in the next chapter, Congress is almost unique among contemporary legislatures in the extent of the power it wields, not least over the executive and its bureaucracy. This situation ensures that cabinet members not only look to the legislature and its committees as much as, or even more than, they do to the president for support for their department projects, but also that cabinet members compete with each other to secure congressional funding and support for 'their' departments and federal agencies.

Furthermore, the federal executive also contains numerous agencies other than the departments of state, over whose structure, composition and personnel the president often has much less formal control. In particular a number of Independent Regulatory Commissions (IRCs) have been established by Congress both to regulate important areas of industrial and commercial activity and to maintain some independence from the presidency. For example the Federal Reserve Board, known as 'the Fed', controls monetary policy, which makes it a vital institution for economic policy-making. In recent years its chairmen have pursued, sometimes against presidential wishes, 'tight money' policies which, in turn, have kept US interest rates consistently high. As Alan Grant comments, 'Presidents have to learn to live with "the Fed" knowing that even though they do not directly control it, the Board will have important effects on the success of their economic strategies.'[14] The 'independent' status of the IRCs is at least theoretically based on the fact that they are administered by boards who are appointed by the president (with senatorial confirmation) for terms which exceed his, and whose composition must be bi-partisan. However, so great is the personnel turnover on the boards of most IRCs that each president usually selects a majority of them on most of the commissions. Consequently, the Supreme Court's decision in 1953 that the president cannot dismiss a commissioner in the way that he can dismiss other political appointees in the executive branch has become increasingly important.

In order to counteract the divisive tendencies inherent in an increasingly institutionally complex and decentralised executive branch of government there has been, again since the 1930s, an enormous growth in the advisory staff of the presidency. This staff, all personally appointed by the president, increased from 1,098 in 1940 to 5,722 in 1972, although by 1981 it had been reduced to the more manageable proportions of about 1,700 individuals. Members are located within the Executive Office of the President, which dates from 1939, and which includes, among a number of important advisory organisations, the president's closest aides and political advisers who collectively form the White House Office. These members of the president's personal staff, usually termed 'special assistants to the president', have also increased substantially in number, from 63 in 1940 to 351 in 1980, under President Carter, and 378 under President Reagan in 1981, with a high point reached in the early 1970s under President Nixon when the White House Office actually exceeded 500 members. The intention behind the creation of the Executive Ofice – 'The President needs help' – was to increase his control over this thoroughly divided – 'atomised' is the term frequently, and not altogether inaccurately, used – executive branch in general, and over the departments of state in particular. However, the reality has been different. Although the large numbers of 'the President's men' now enable them to duplicate and to monitor, and theoretically to control, the activities of both the executive departments and the other institutions of the executive branch, the outcome has simply been to make the president more rather than less distant from these departments. In particular, as Professor Blondel stresses, 'the effect has been to create a second (or first) government which forms a screen between President and Cabinet,'[15] effectively dividing governmental institutions, personnel and authority to an extent which is unique among contemporary regimes.

3 Contemporary Legislatures

The development, spread and decline of parliaments

As the tripartite governmental division of institutions (if not exactly of labour or functions) developed, representative assemblies and parliaments, which progressively broke away from executives in the early modern period in Europe, eventually emerged as modern legislatures. Today legislative institutions are widely, but, in direct contrast to the ubiquitous executive, by no means universally distributed among contemporary regimes. A survey which excluded states of less than one million population found that in 1981 93 states claimed a legislature of some sort, whilst 33 states, most of which were military regimes, had none.[1] In the latter group of states legislative responsibilities are absorbed by the executive, as they were in the states of medieval Europe. Nevertheless in the majority of contemporary regimes executives and legislatures exist as separate institutions, characteristically sharing, albeit to widely varying degrees and in very different ways, legislative powers and functions between them. Thus, a detailed survey conducted in 1971 found that only five states (all in the Middle East) had never had a legislature, and that only four other states had spent the whole of the previous decade without any assembly at all.[2]

Although these 'representative' institutions are referred to by a number of terms – ranging from the title 'legislature' (commonly and correctly used in the USA), to the anglophone idea of 'parliament' and its francophone counterpart the 'assembly', as well as of other less common synonyms such as 'diet' – all of these terms have a similar connotation of 'an institution meeting to deliberate'.[3] Moreover, these deliberations are frequently focussed on the process of law-making. Whilst no legislature possesses an exclusive control over this process, legislatures commonly have an important formal role to play, in that laws tend to require enactment by the legislature. This makes variations in institutional responsibility for this process very much one of degree. Indeed, since policy-making cannot in practice be conveniently separated into law-making and law-implementing, neat and convenient divisions between legislatures making laws and executives carrying them out are absent in all contemporary regimes. 'As a result, legislatures and executives are separate institutions sharing policy making in different proportions in different countries.'[4]

The 'golden age' of legislatures occurred in the nineteenth century. Governments were then responsible for only a limited range of domestic and foreign policies. Consequently large multi-member assemblies could convincingly assert their deliberative as well as their democratic and representative strengths against frequently less popular, less democratic and less representative executives. In contrast, however, the twentieth century has frequently been said to have been 'hard on legislatures'. As governments have increasingly sought to involve themselves in and to control social and economic activities that previously were left to market forces the workloads expected of parliaments have expanded enormously. Similarly their impact on social and economic life, through the legislation they have sponsored and passed, has also vastly increased. However, what has not increased to the same degree has been the impact of legislatures on policy-making. This century has seen a *relative* 'decline of parliaments' in terms of their impact (in terms of both form and content) on the making of important political decisions. This decline is matched by and reflected in the increasing impact of the executive, both political and bureaucratic, as well as in the rising significance of non-governmental organisations in the form of organised parties and pressure groups.

As executives became increasingly democratically accountable institutions – either through the adoption of an American-style directly elected presidency or, in parliamentary regimes, through the emergence of a British-style highly disciplined party system – they acquired political resources which enabled them to compete with legislatures as institutions of popular representation. This trend towards executive supremacy could be more easily constitutionally and legally sanctioned and ensured in presidential systems with their more or less strict separation of legislative and executive personnel. However, the actual impact of a combination of party majorities and party discipline in parliaments led, in practice, to precisely the same kind of result in parliamentary regimes. Moreover, this twentieth-century trend towards executive rather than parliamentary government was further reinforced by the enormous increases in the quantity as well as the complexity of the political responsibilities undertaken by contemporary regimes. Representation, either by individuals or through organised national political parties, proved to be insufficient for executives to gain the necessary specialised information or to gauge the reactions of affected segments of the population as they sought to make political choices and to plan future policies. The upshot has been an almost global trend towards national bargaining between major pressure groups and, particularly, the organisations representing the employers and the employed on the one hand, and the 'permanent government', the executive bureaucracy, on the other; negotiations which frequently by-pass parliament altogether.

Thus, executives in most contemporary regimes appear to have regained much of the power they gradually lost to legislatures over earlier centuries. Characteristically executives now undertake the crucial activities of planning and formulating new legislative proposals, as well as their conventionally executive functions of applying and implementing the resultant laws. Additionally, in many regimes, executives are able to secure the enactment of these proposals substantially unaltered by the nominal 'legislature'. Thus, in practice, contemporary legislatures are only in rare and isolated cases 'strong' or powerful political institutions in terms of their decision and policy-making responsibilities. If 'strong' is defined in terms of the ability to prevent the executive making policy unilaterally, only three contemporary legislatures can be so described, the Congresses of the USA and Costa Rica and the Italian Parliament.[5] In most other cases far from actually legislating, parliaments in the present century often appear to have been reduced to playing seemingly minor, and sometimes minimal or even purely symbolic roles in the political life of contemporary regimes.

Legislatures: contemporary functions and impact

In 1971 approximately 90 per cent of the states of the economically developed North, 90 per cent of Asian and Latin American states, 70 per cent of African states and 50–60 per cent of those in the Middle East, possessed legislatures. These figures underline the point that such institutions are too widespread and too persistent to be automatically defined as politically unimportant in contemporary regimes.[6] However, the political impact of most of these institutions differs from that suggested by earlier definitions of legislatures as bodies elected by the people at relatively frequent intervals to make laws. Modern parliaments also belie the attendant assumption that representative governments are built around legislatures which translate public desires into governmental decisions. Except in the most formal of senses, most legislatures no longer make laws. An analysis of over forty legislatures undertaken in the mid-1970s, for example, found that in most of them the executive introduced over 80 per cent of all pieces of legislation, and that a further 80 per cent of these bills were passed. Nevertheless, their lack of policy-making power relative to the executive institutions of government must not obscure the very wide and extensive list of political functions undertaken by legislatures in contemporary regimes – a list which covers far more tasks than unrealistic classical theories centering on legislation alone would allow.

In this sense the idea of legislative 'decline' is rather misleading *except* in terms of control over the making of laws. For contemporary legislatures share – in varying combinations and to varying degrees – with executives, political parties and pressure groups, in such significant activities as:

i) Representing the interests of the public to members of the executive (both political and bureaucratic).

ii) Educating and informing the populace on issues of major importance.

iii) Supervising the operations of bureaucrats.

iv) Often recruiting (and sometimes dismissing) the occupants of posts of major decision-making significance in the political executive.

v) Participating in the creation and maintenance of public support for and confidence in the regime.

From these perspectives it can hardly be asserted that legislatures in general are politically unimportant or insignificant, for they clearly perform important services for contemporary regimes. In fact in carrying out these tasks contemporary legislatures are acting in a manner which is not dissimilar to their original medieval ancestors and counterparts, called by monarchs to publicly test and confirm the acceptability of their proposals. Modern representative assemblies are similarly well suited, in both composition and organisation, to assessing and publicising the acceptability of executive proposals to the wider public.

Almost all legislatures in contemporary governments either possess relatively 'modest' policy-making powers – in the sense that, in practice, they can expect to modify but not to reject outright executive proposals – or possess negligible policy-making powers and are unable either to modify or to reject executive measures.[8] Most of the liberal democratic regimes of the First World can be included among the list of those parliaments possessing 'modest' policy-making powers. The parliaments of Second World states (with the partial exception of Yugoslavia), however, have minimal impacts of policy-making, and they are joined by many Third World legislatures in this 'negligible influence' category.

Nevertheless, the fact that almost all the world's legislatures appear to play a relatively weak or merely a formal role in policy-making, should not automatically lead one to assume that they have little or no overall legislative impact on the executive. If law-making has become an essentially executive function, the same cannot be said for what is often called the 'control function' of parliaments. Almost all legislatures are organised for some form of scrutiny of the executive. Parliamentary systems charateristically have some form of question time, whilst, in both parliamentary and presidential regimes, committees seek to investigate executive (including bureaucratic) activities and personnel as well as policies. Similarly, parliamentary debates may themselves influence both the ideas and the activities of executives.

Furthermore, parliaments are representative assemblies, composed of elected members, and are important contexts through which public opinion, as well as the more specific opinions of organised groups, can be focussed on matters of public concern. Similarly, individual members of parliament are expected to use their privileged representative status to secure access to governmental institutions and members, and to engage in 'errand-running' for their constituents. Activities such as these take up much of the efforts and time of parliaments and their members. They range from dealing with complaints about bureaucratic inertia, inefficiency and corruption, through special pleading to bureaucrats on behalf of constituents, to attempts to secure preferential treatment for their constituencies when funds are allocated for relevant purposes. 'Much of the work,' for example, of the Members of Parliament in the East African state of Kenya, 'consists of running constituents' errands,' and a study undertaken in 1974 showed that 82 per cent of them were primarily concerned with constituency problems and with obtaining resources and favours for their constituents from the executive. Their re-election depends on their success in fulfilling these expectations.[9]

Similarly, and again irrespective of their impacts on policy-making, parliaments can make important contributions toward the levels of stability (or its converse) achieved by individual regimes. First, the fact that legislative service is generally seen as a useful and sometimes, as in Britain, essential, preparation for the achievement of executive office, ensures that parliaments generally play important functions in recruiting national political élites and leaders and developing a shared political outlook among them. Second, the existence of a body of legislators with shared political values may enable parliamentarians to solve conflicts, or keep them within acceptable limits, thereby contributing to the stability of their states. Conversely, of course, legislatures may also exacerbate rather than defuse conflicts, if the disputes between the different segments (ethnic, regional, or ideological) of the population represented run deep and are not counterbalanced by equally powerful impulses towards compromise and consensus. Innumerable examples have occurred, are occurring and will continue to occur of legislatures which have contributed to governmental instability by forcing executives to resign because of a loss of legislative support. In many other cases legislatures have contributed to the demise not just of governments but of regimes, and in a few recent cases, of states and political communities, when the underlying national consensus breaks down and agreed institutional arrangements are abandoned.

Third, in all contemporary regimes, democratic and authoritarian, the major function of legislatures can be viewed as legitimising the actions of the regime. Thus, in authoritarian and one-party systems members of parliament are required to explain and defend governmental policies in their constituencies, and in democratic regimes members may (according to the party composition of the executive) seek to do so. Moreover, the form, if not always the substance, of legislative participation in the law-making process appears to be a universal expectation held by both domestic and international publics. Legislatures generally appear to serve important functions as symbols of popular participation in politics and this aura appears to give them a legitimacy often denied to other political institutions.

The Soviet and American legislatures provide, between them, examples of the parameters within which the policy-making powers and political impact of parliamentary institutions in contemporary regimes can vary – from, in the case of the US Congress, an uniquely powerful institution vis-a-vis the executive, to, in the case of the Supreme Soviet of the USSR, one with comparatively insignificant and muted political impact.

Case study: The USSR Supreme Soviet

Like the legislative institutions in other Second World, and in many Third World, one-party states, the Supreme Soviet of the USSR has a minimal impact on policy-making and very limited political influence compared to that exercised by the ruling Communist party and by the Soviet bureaucracy. However, paradoxically, the political impact of the Supreme Soviet has clearly grown since the death of Stalin and particularly since the removal of Nikita Khrushchev in 1964, and there are indications that its political status is continuing to rise in the 1980s. Thus, the Soviet legislature appears to offer a counter-example, if only a limited one, to the 'normal' twentieth-century trend of legislatures continually and consistently losing power to executives.

As befits a legislature in a federal system, the Supreme Soviet of the USSR is bicameral. The constituencies for these two chambers are very different. The Council of the Union is composed according to population with one deputy for every 300,000 people. For the Council of Nationalities (the federal chamber) there is geographical representation for the different national groups that comprise the Soviet Union, via a form of proportional representation. Otherwise the two chambers are equal in rights and equal in size, each being composed of 750 deputies. Each Supreme Soviet is elected for five years and constitutionally must meet at least twice per annum. Otherwise extraordinary sessions can be called. Great care is taken by the ruling Communist party, which controls nominations and elections, to make the Supreme Soviet broadly representative of the population of the USSR. Whilst over 70 per cent of deputies are party members (71.7 per cent in 1984) this reflects a slow but steady decline from the situation in the early 1950s when 83.5 per cent of deputies were party members. Moreover, apart from this increase in the proportion of non-party members, there has also been a steady increase in the representation of women, workers and peasants, and young people.

What then are the functions of the Supreme Soviet? Constitutionally the Supreme Soviet is a legislature – termed 'The highest body of state authority . . . empowered to deal with all matters within the jurisdiction of the USSR . . .' by the 1977 constitution (Article 108) – but in practice it is a legislature only in a very formal sense. The Supreme Soviet rarely meets more than twice in a year, and sometimes less, and these sessions last only a few days and always less than one week. Clearly then, most legislative work, such as preparing, drafting, and amending proposed legislation, occurs outside the full sessions of the Supreme Soviet. Further, there is no real debate in the full Supreme Soviet; it is essentially a declaratory and ratifying body which simply sets the seal on decisions which have been prepared, drafted and made elsewhere. Significantly, over many decades (apart from three disagreements on procedure in 1938) there has been no recorded instance of any decision of the full Supreme Soviet which has not been totally unanimous, and since

1936 only a single abstention has been recorded, and that was, apparently, accidental. In practice, the time of full sessions of the Supreme Soviet is spent on a series of speeches, receptions and occasional voting, with the legislature passing approximately 10 laws per session and averaging 21 laws per annum since 1970. 'The responsibilities of the Supreme Soviet deputy, one elected, are not unduly onerous,' Stephen White wryly observes, and the time taken up by plenary sessions does not normally preclude the deputies from getting in 'a good day's shopping while in the capital . . . .'[10] Moreover, these sessions are, in practice, more like the relatively relaxed and informal atmosphere of the House of Commons than brief glimpses on British television of seas of attentive faces and imposing arrays of raised arms during unanimous votes would suggest. As the *New York Times* recorded, 'Some of the deputies listened attentively. Some read *Pravda* . . . Many, by chatting among themselves, created a buzz when speakers on the rostrum drew a breath, or yielded to their successors. A few deputies appeared to be asleep.'[11] The more important of the two annual meetings is probably the one which takes place towards the end of the year, usually in December, and invariably considers the annual budget and the national one- and five-year Economic Plans. Since the 1950s, sessions have been concerned less with broad questions of foreign policy and more with domestic social, economic and constitutional matters. Following these brief sessions the full Supreme Soviet goes into recess, and the deputies return to their constituencies and to full-time jobs, with Supreme Soviet work being viewed very much as a part-time activity for its members. Indeed, the sessions of the full Supreme Soviet underline an important principle of Soviet political life, namely that if an institution meets in public, debate will be minimal or non-existent and decisions will be unanimous.

Like almost all other contemporary legislatures the Supreme Soviet has a well-developed committee system. In the mid-1960s there were ten commissions in each house of the Soviet legislature covering such fields as planning and the budget, agriculture, legislative proposals and foreign affairs. By 1970 there were twenty-six of these commissions, thirteen in each chamber, and a number of subordinate sub-committees. By 1980 the number had increased to sixteen in each chamber. Commissions are appointed for the whole five-year life of the Supreme Soviet, and they meet more frequently and sit longer than the parent body. Additionally, they act privately with at least some degree of access to persons and papers. Consequently, the commissions are in a position at least to be able to influence the details of legislation and as they meet in private they can debate. In practice it seems that these standing commissions have played an increasing preparatory role in Soviet law-making in recent years, both engaging in 'consulation' with the public and with relevant experts and also assisting in the drafting of proposed legislation. Indeed, the expansion of the activities of the commissions is probably the best practical example of the increasing role of the Supreme Soviet in the legislative process – a tendency which has been noticeable since the mid-1960s.

By 1980, 76 per cent of Supreme Soviet deputies were involved in committee work. However, closer analysis is instructive, for there are two major groups in any Supreme Soviet. First, there is a large minority group of relatively permanent members, significantly dominated by Communist party and government officials, and a majority group of transient members. This reflects the fact that approximately two-thirds of deputies serve only one term. Significantly, the permanent group occupies on average a majority of seats on the commissions. Equally significantly, whereas almost 30 per cent of members of the full Supreme Soviet are not party members, very few committee members are not. The explanation is simple. As the committees have come to play a more significant role in the preparation and investigation of policy proposals the party has increasingly sought to keep a tight control over their activities. Moreover, it is important to remember the limitations under which committees of the Soviet legislature work. In complete contrast, for example, to those of the American Congress, these committees have no permanent staff and therefore depend on other agencies, and in particular on the goodwill of the Soviet bureaucratic agencies under the control of the Council of Ministers, to gain information and to provide specialist advisors. Nevertheless, up to 300 outside consultants and experts are usually engaged for committee investigations of items of major importance such as the annual examination of the economic Plan and the Soviet budget.

Overall, it appears that these standing commissions perform three functions. First, they examine, amend and approve the annual budget and economic plan for the USSR, and, since 1971, the five-year plans too, as well as, since 1978, reports on the fulfilment of these economic plans and on budgetary performance. The outcome is, characteristically, an acceptance by the full Supreme Soviet of the government's broad budgetary and planning proposals, but with a number of amendments in line with the changes proposed by the planning-budget commissions. These amendments are, in the context of the overall budget, relatively minor (always less than 1 per cent of total expenditure in recent years). However, the careful analysis of the available data by Stephen White also highlights a consistent tendency for the Supreme Soviet deputies to support, and to win, increased government expenditure on social and cultural matters, such as schools, hospitals, libraries, kindergartens, sports facilities and welfare benefits. Clearly these are precisely the items of expenditure which one would logically expect Soviet constituents to press their deputies to achieve. Nevertheless it is impossible, given the secretive nature of the Soviet system, to conclude that these changes in budgetary emphasis 'occurred', as White points out, 'only and exclusively because of the influence of the Supreme Soviet towards that end.'[12] Second, the standing commissions can (but rarely do) initiate legislation, and propose amendments to draft legislation submitted by the government. This latter task of scrutiny is, in practice, actively pursued, and the commissions are assisted in this task by consultations with academic institutions and other specialist bodies, as well as by public debate and the characteristically heavy public correspondence that follows the announcement of proposed legislation. As a result, few pieces of legislation are unchanged, and the changes may be large. Third, the commissions exercise the function of *kontrol* over the government. This supervisory and monitoring activity include examining ministerial performance and their observance of their legislative obligations. Following investigations, recommendations are made to eliminate any shortcomings unearthed – processes similar to those which occur in most modern parliaments.

Moreover, the expanded role of the commissions has been

accompanied, over the last decade or so, by generally improved conditions and increased rights and benefits for deputies of the Supreme Soviet under legislation passed since the mid-1960s. Overall, these developments suggest the Soviet legislature's impact is perhaps rather greater than that of the 'rubber stamp' which is all the influence many distinguished academics were prepared to concede to it until recently.[13] Certainly recent chairmen of the USSR Supreme Soviet have publicly stressed the need for the legislature to have genuine authority over the Soviet government and the Soviet bureaucracy and increasingly to control, in a meaningful way, the activities of the Council of Ministers and its subordinate ministries. It will be very interesting to see what progress in this direction the future actually brings.

Case study: the US Congress

Like the Supreme Soviet of the USSR, and for the same reason, the US Congress is bicameral, with the 435 representatives in the House of Representatives elected from congressional districts varying in population between 400 and 650,000, and the one hundred senators in the Senate elected on the basis of two per state, irrespective of population. Broadly, the two chambers are equal in power, but Senators who are elected for six years, compared to the Representatives' two, have greater status, better facilities and more staff. Under the constitution, Congress is given a high degree of autonomy from the executive, with the two houses free to decide exactly how to organise and arrange their affairs in order to carry out their responsibilities as the legislative branch of government. Moreover, the constitution also grants a high degree of authority to the legislature, notably the 'power of the purse'. This determines that money for the executive branch can *only* be provided by appropriations bills duly passed by Congress, giving the latter a high degree of control over financial and budgetary matters – including control over funds appropriated for Congress's own budgetary requirements. Additionally, declarations of war, must, according to the constitution, emanate from Congress. Furthermore, the Senate is given a specific responsibility to 'advise and consent' to treaties entered into by the executive branch and to a wide range of presidential appointments, including Supreme Court justices and Cabinet members. The president can, in his turn, veto bills passed by Congress, although this veto can also be overridden by a two-thirds majority of congressmen.

Thus, Congress possesses, compared to other contemporary legislatures, an unusually high degree of institutional and organisational independence from the executive, as well as a great deal of political authority and influence. However, the significant point is that this political power is not exercised *independently* of the executive branch. On the contrary, whilst presidency and Congress remain strictly *separated* institutions in terms of organisation and personnel, the two branches of government are forced by the constitution to share the powers and responsibilities for legislation and government between them. Consequently, whilst president and Congress must co-operate to create laws and to process the budgetary and financial needs of the federal government, the constitution had also ensured that perpetual legislative-executive conflict and competition is automatically and deliberately built into the governmental process.

While the nineteenth century mainly witnessed (as the framers of the constitution clearly intended) what Woodrow Wilson termed 'congressional government', with only relatively brief periods of executive dominance, this situation has been reversed during the present century, and, most particularly since the 1930s. With the Depression, and the flood of 'New Deal' legislation which followed during the presidency of F. D. Roosevelt, the executive branch became, and has remained, the major initiator of legislation. Since 1933 Congress has become dependent on a comprehensive annual legislative programme presented by the president. Moreover, the increase in presidential power associated with increasing governmental involvement in the economy was further reinforced by the rising importance of foreign policy, from 1941 when the USA finally rejected global isolationism and entered the Second World War. Indeed, it was the arena of foreign policy, with its constant wartime and post-war 'emergencies' and 'crises' which most clearly underlined the point that one president could make important and often urgent decisions more effectively and rapidly than 535 congressmen. Congress, on the other hand, was well-equipped to deal with the particulars and detail of government and to play checking, critical, controlling and investigatory roles. Consequently, with the complete acquiescence of the legislature, an agreed division of labour between executive branch and legislative branch emerged in the years following the Second World War.

As a result of this implicitly accepted division of labour, the organisation of Congress developed in a direction compatible with its concentration on controlling the detail of policies which had been assembled, co-ordinated and presented by the presidency. In particular, in order to effectively undertake its tasks of amending, delaying and (in some residual areas of policy) initiating legislation to fill the perceived gaps in the president's otherwise comprehensive legislative programme, Congress increasingly organised itself in a decentralised manner through the expansion of its committee and its sub-committee system. Within this decentralised structure each congressman examined the presidential legislative programme mainly, in the absence of a disciplined party system, from the perspective of their individual constituencies. 'The President proposed, from the national perspective, and the Congress disposed, from the perspective of an aggregate of separate constituencies.'[14]

Committees, in turn, are the institutional means through which the congressman can 'earn' his re-election through service to constituents who judge his performance in Washington principally on the basis of his success in attracting federal money and federal jobs, through what is known as 'pork barrel' legislation, to his district or state. Significantly, an election-day poll in 1978 revealed that of three factors which might influence their vote for a congressman, 47 per cent chose 'what you think he can do for this community', 36 per cent 'because of his stand on national issues', and 17 per cent 'because you respect him as a person'.[15] Small wonder, then, that congressmen seek membership on those committees of particular relevance to their constituencies or that are particularly important in determining federal spending. An old, but true, congressional story has the chairman of the Naval Affairs Committee asked, 'Is it not a fact that the navy yard in your district will not accommodate our latest battleships?' and answering, 'That is true, and that is the reason I have always been in favour of small ships.'[16] As a result of these insidious constituency pressures congress has become an incurably and inevitably parochial institution, and one which is congenitally incapable of adopting the broad national perspective forced on the President by his nation-wide constituency.

Furthermore, the individualism which overriding constituency pressures fostered has in turn caused an increasing fragmentation and dispersal of political authority within the legislature – a dispersal which is particularly difficult to counteract due to the weakness of party ties and party discipline in the USA. Indeed, voting patterns are one of the best indications of the individualistic behaviour of congressmen. For, whilst the party label remains the best single indicator of the way a congressman will vote, the number of votes (roll calls) in any Congress on which a majority of the members of the two parties vote against each other is well under 50 per cent. If British standards of party voting are applied, the proportion of votes on which strict partisan divisions occur never exceeds 10 per cent. Almost invariably between 20 and 30 per cent of congressmen will vote against their 'own' party. Additionally, to complicate the issue still further, American voters have chosen a Republican president in five of the last three elections held – between 1956 and 1984 – while at each of these elections a Democratic House of Representatives was returned and, with the exception of the 1980 and 1984 elections, a Democratic Senate too.

Party ties and party discipline in Congress have also become weaker rather than stronger since the 1960s, with individualistic voting increasing correspondingly. Until the early 1970s, some organisational cohesion – albeit at the expense of placing power in the hands of a relatively small number of congressmen from particularly safe seats – was provided in Congress by the principle of 'seniority' (i.e. length of service) as the main criterion for deciding the all-important question of committee assignments and chairmanships. While party replaced seniority in the 1970s as the main criteria for committee placements, party leadership in Congress was not, in practice, strengthened as a result. For while Congress maintains a formal structure of party institutions and a hierarchy of party leaders, the influence of these institutions and individuals over issues other than organisational questions is small in comparison with that of their counterparts in most other legislatures. In particular their influence over voting

patterns is usually negligible. Moreover, congressional individualism and organisational decentralisation has been further reinforced by the astonishing proliferation of sub-committees. By the
mid-1970s these sub-committees had frequently become the real
centres of power and influence in an increasingly decentralised
Congress. By 1976 the average representative had six committee and sub-committee posts and the average senator eighteen.
Since then, there has been some rationalisation, particularly in
the Senate where the numbers of both sub-committees and
committees were markedly reduced in the late 1970s. Thus, while
Congress supported a grand total of 54 standing committees and
269 sub-committees in 1978, by 1981 the figures were 37 and
(approximately) 220 – still uniquely high in comparative terms.
Moreover, congressmen and their committees and sub-committees are supported by uniquely large funds and uniquely large
professional staffs, particularly since what has been termed an
'explosion' of new staff posts created in the mid-1970s.[17] Consequently Congress now employs a grand total of over 30,000
individuals. In comparison, the second most generously staffed
of the world's legislatures, the Canadian parliament, employs
about 3,300 people.

That Congress was in the 1970s by far the fastest growing
branch of the US government, reflected the fact that after a long
period of executive ascendancy, particularly in the foreign policy
field, the legislature was increasingly reasserting its authority over
the presidency. In the hands of Richard Nixon (elected in 1968
and re-elected in 1972) the presidency had finally discredited
itself morally and politically, both over its handling of governmental leadership – notably the undeclared Vietnam war – and
over the control, or lack of control, over its own personal staff
– underlined by the curious events surrounding the Watergate
scandal. Paradoxically, however, owing to its organisational
decentralisation and its in-built parochialism, this resurgent
Congress rapidly proved institutionally incapable of providing the
kind of national leadership and co-ordination of policy and legislation previously provided by the presidency. This inherent
inability to develop coherent legislative programmes, or even to
respond to executive actions as an united institution, clearly
limits congressional capacity to replace the presidency as the

driving and initiating force in the political process.

Not surprisingly, therefore, before the end of the 1970s, congressmen and the American public were already calling for a return to presidential leadership. Thus, after a relatively short cycle of congressional primacy during the 1970s, the election of a Republican president, Ronald Reagan, in 1980 on a platform featuring strong executive leadership, appeared to presage the start of a new cycle of increasing presidential primacy, and a corresponding decline of Congress. Commentators on the contemporary Congress, despite recognising its unique effectiveness as a legislature always return to the problems of decentralisation – of an institution 'caught between the Scylla of excessive attention to legislative-administrative detail and the Charybdis of inadequate focus on the foundations of broader policy directions.'[18] Small wonder, then, that a perceptive American public consistently values its individual congressmen more highly than it does Congress as an institution. Congress is expected by Americans to solve national problems, and is generally considered to be doing this badly. Its members are expected to solve more immediate constituency problems, and are perceived to be doing this consistently well.

4 Political Centralisation and Decentralisation: The Nature of Federalism and Federal Government

Decentralisation and its institutional forms

The classification of governments and constitutions into federal (decentralised) and unitary (centralised) forms has a long and distinguished pedigree, and it remains a useful basis on which to begin an analysis of patterns of political centralisation and decentralisation among contemporary regimes. However, all governments, no matter how centralised, need at the very least to delegate responsibility for the execution and implementation of their centrally-decided policies to regional or locally-based branches or organisations. Furthermore, many governments, mindful of one or both of the twin pressures of democracy and efficiency, make some attempt to decentralise at least some of the functions of government.

Decentralisation can therefore take any one of a number of different institutional forms (Figure 1.1). These form a continuum which commences with the simple delegation of administrative tasks by the policy-making central government to what are termed the 'field services' of this central government. A further stage of decentralisation is achieved through the type of statutory donation of powers to local authorities found in Britain. Beyond this the continuum progresses to the conditional and reversible devolution of authority to regional assemblies, and thence to the permanent and constitutional division of functions and authority of federalism. Finally the continuum arrives at such loose confederal or supra-national alliances of independent states as the European Economic Community (EEC) in which central decision-making depends on the wishes of the member governments, rather than those of the Community institutions. Within these parameters an infinite variety of hybrid forms and sub-types are possible. Most importantly the place of any country on the

Figure 4.1   Forms of decentralisation

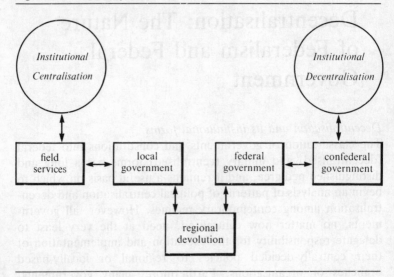

continuum may vary quite markedly over time. Different regimes, or indeed the same regimes, frequently seek to vary the structure or the influence of their territorially based institutions of government, and therefore alter the geographical balance of political power and influence in the state. For example the nation states of Western Europe are currently facing what has aptly been termed 'erosion' from both 'above' and from 'below'.[1] The erosion from 'above' reflects the pressures towards trans-nationalism and the impact of supra-national organisations which have developed in the region, particularly in the aftermath of the Second World War. In practice, those fears frequently expressed in Britain, over the dangers of a loss of sovereignty and independence to international organisations, and particularly the EEC, have resulted in the domination of European Community decision-making by the member governments. As a result the supra-national Community institutions remain relatively weak, currently leaving the Community as an alliance or an association of independent states rather than as an emergent trans-national federation.

The geographical distribution of power within the mainly centralised and unitary states of Western Europe – only three, Austria, Switzerland and West Germany are fully federal – has also been frequently challenged from 'below' of recent years, not least in Britain. The causes of 'sub-state' nationalism – exemplified by the rise of nationalism in both Scotland and Wales, with its attendant pressures towards regionalism and/or autonomy – are varied, and differ from state to state. At the same time these pressures were everywhere associated with the same sense of dissatisfaction with traditional forms and styles of government that led to the development of trans-national organisations such as the EEC.

In general however, despite such pressures from 'below' urging decentralisation, the mainly centralised and unitary states of Western Europe have resisted fundamental shifts in the territorial division of power – just as they have successfully resisted the pressures towards trans-national government. These states – Britain is a prime example – have responded by considering and in some cases implementing forms of administrative deconcentration and decentralisation. Nonetheless, the overall impact has not been great. Most European states remain firmly within the centralised and unitary segment of the spectrum. However, as the British case also highlights, the arguments and the administrative experiments and reforms are likely to continue into the future. Thus, while it is theoretically possible to place any government on a scale or a continuum running from institutional centralisation to institutional decentralisation, this ascription must always be viewed as a temporary one.

Federalism
Different authorities are prone to define the different segments of this hypothetical continuum in very different ways. For example, the word federalism has been applied to a very wide variety of very different forms of government, from centralised dictatorships to loose alliances, and from highly successful to very fragile political systems. Consequently the number of cases in a particular category of decentralisation often varies widely, both as a result of varying definitions and due to variations in the strictness with which similar definitions are applied. Thus, in the

Table 4.1   Federal governments: two interpretations

K. C. Wheare	W. H. Riker	
Australia	Argentina	Mexico
Canada	Australia	Nigeria
Switzerland	Austria	Pakistan
USA	Brazil	Soviet Union
	Cameroon	Switzerland
Total 4	Canada	Tanzania
	Czechoslovakia	United States
	Germany	Venezuela
	India	Yugoslavia
	Malaysia	
		Total 19

Source: K. C. Wheare, *Federal Government* Oxford University Press, 4th ed, 1963.

Source: W. H. Riker, 'Federalism', in F. I. Greenstein & N. Polsby, (ed), *Handbook of Political Science*, vol 5, Addison-Wesley, 1975, pp. 93–172.

case of federalism, one eminent authority finds only four modern examples of genuinely federal governments, and another finds a total of nineteen (see Table 4.1). What is agreed by all authorities is that the global pattern of centralisation and decentralisation parallels that of Western Europe in that the great majority of the world's states claim to be unitary. In fact only about twenty of the world's states currently claim (or have until recently claimed) to be federal. In these states the constitutions generally guarantee that 'the activities of government are divided between regional government and a central government in such a way that each kind of government has some activities on which it makes final decisions.' These constitutional arrangements are intended to deal with the problems presented by territorial diversity by providing 'a degree of regional autonomy and systematic national representation for geographically distinct units.'[2] Such institutional arrangements are designed to allow the constituent regions or states to maintain control over their own immediate affairs whilst at the same time giving the central or federal government control over those issues and activities which the constituent units agree to be of general concern.

Significantly, these twenty or so states cover between them more than half the land surface of the world. The governments of all really large territories, with the sole exception of China, describe themselves as federations. Clearly, therefore, federations are few but qualitatively important. Indeed, since many of these federations are of relatively recent vintage, there is even some justification for describing the present era as an age of federalism. For federalism can be seen as the main alternative and successor to empire as a method for combining large areas under one government. Consequently it became a fashionable solution to one of the major political problems of decolonisation following the Second World War – how to combine the benefits of unity and diversity in the many large, heterogeneous and randomly-defined territories emerging into independence in the postwar era.

Modern federalism was devised at the Philadelphia Convention which gave birth to the United States of America in 1787 – superseding the older style of federation or alliance of independent states, uniting for limited purposes such as defence. Since them it has been adopted as a form of government by Switzerland, Canada, Australia, a number of Latin American states, the USSR, Yugoslavia, West Germany and Austria, as well as by India, Pakistan, Malaysia and Nigeria. Equally there have been a large number of failed federations, particularly in Central and South America and the Caribbean, as well as in Africa. This situation is reflected in the assumption made by many commentators that federalism is an inherently unstable form of government, tending to move inexorably either towards disintegration or full centralisation.

Unsurprisingly, therefore, there is a general expectation in the literature on federalism that, to quote one commentator, 'the path of federalism never runs smoothly.'[3] In particular there is an assumption that federal systems with their multiple levels of government and their complicated methods of decision-making – designed to ensure the assent of all their territorial units and component parts – find it inherently more difficult to adjust to changing circumstances than their more centralised, and therefore more flexible, counterparts. This problem is seen as becoming steadily more acute in the context of a rapidly changing world. Indeed, the mixed fate of federal government in Nigeria – suspended in the late 1960s after a bloody civil war, re-established in 1979, and suspended again at the end of 1983 by another military coup – epitomises the mixed fate of federalism globally in the past decade or so. The establishment of the new state of Bangladesh (formerly East Pakistan) by civil war and secession brought the end of any hope of federation between the two Pakistans in 1971. Bangladesh itself rejected federalism, and whilst a new federalism was established in (West) Pakistan in 1973 this also succumbed to a military coup in 1977. Federalism was also abruptly terminated in the Africa state of Cameroon in 1972. Elsewhere, however, the outlook has seemed brighter for federalism. Belgium, with its acute linguistic and communal problems, has been moving steadily towards overt federalism over the last decade or so. The United Arab Emirates in the Persian Gulf formed a federation in December 1971 (albeit on principles more feudal than democratic). A military coup in the Gambia in 1981 inaugurated a formal process of confederal union (Senegambia) between that tiny state and Senegal which surrounds and dominates it, geographically and economically. Similarly, in 1982, Egypt and the Sudan concluded another of the Middle East's numerous (and almost all short-lived) federal or confederal agreements, in the form of a Charter of Integration between the two states. Finally, 1984 saw the inauguration of a federal form of agreement between Libya and Morocco.

Federalism and decentralisation. A simple assumption underpins much of the writing on the question of federalism. Federalism is assumed to be an institutional response to societal divisions and diversities, with the 'federal' nature of the society at least roughly reflected in the forms of its constitutional and political arrangements (federalism). From this perspective, all societies can be placed on a continuum running from (in theory only) wholly integrated and undivided to wholly divided and diversified. The major social divisions which in turn define the 'federalness' of a particular society, are ethnic, national and linguistic, with religious, economic, geographical and historical divisions playing a supportive role. Federalism then becomes an institutional mechanism through which the balance between the forces for unity (centralisation) and diversity (decentralisation) may be institutionalised. The territorially divided and geographically separated institutions of a federal government are seen as potentially providing channels for inter-regional and inter-group communication, for delaying precipitate decisions and actions, and for offering an institutional context within which acceptable compromises can be achieved. The resultant form of government will therefore be more or less federal according to the relative and shifting strengths of the two opposing demands: for unity or for diversity, for integration or for disintegration. Thus, the essence of federalism perhaps lies less in terms of its impact on levels of decentralisation or centralisation than in its concern to recognise the existence and the importance of territorial divisions in a society. In short, federalism provides for a decision-making process that underlines the relevance of territorially-based loyalties.

Federalism implies that the autonomy of regional governments cannot be removed by the central government without their consent. This does not mean that the share of power held by the regional governments will be very extensive. Thus there may be only a rather limited value in the traditional classificatory distinction between federal and unitary systems of government. It is impossible to assume that a state terming itself federal will automatically be more decentralised in the *practice* – as opposed to the theory – of its government and politics than a state claiming to be unitary. Moreover, contemporary conditions, and particularly economic factors, have led to ever greater interdependence among the different levels of government in federal systems, with the different levels of government sharing in the various tasks of government. This situation makes it impossible to neatly divide responsibilities between central and territorial governments in the way that federal theory seems to demand. Closely related to this integration of different levels of government is a tendency towards the centralisation of governmental decision-making in all federal systems. In particular, in every federal system the control which has fallen to the central government over financial matters has given these governments a dominant impact in relation to their territorial, and now subordinate, counterparts.

It is also vitally important to stress that the degree of political centralisation – that is the extent to which political decision-making is in the hands of the central government – varies very widely between different federal states. The Soviet Union, by common consent, can be classified as a highly centralised federation, as can Yugoslavia and Mexico. On the other hand, there are a number of less centralised federations such as Canada and Australia, the United States, and possibly India. In these states many important political decisions are still made by the territorial governments and the idea of state, regional or provincial rights remains very meaningful. These variations in degrees of centralisation between different federations appear to correspond very closely to levels of centralisation in their party systems. In the highly centralised federations – the Soviet Union, Yugoslavia and Mexico – the party system, in each case dominated by a single party, is also highly centralised. Similarly, in Austria – although the party system here is competitive – highly centralised national parties have fundamentally influenced the impact of constitutional federalism. Conversely, in the less highly centralised federations the political party system is also more decentralised. This correlation holds good not only for the competitive party systems found in the United States, Canada and Australia, but also, more surprisingly, for India. Here – despite a large concentration of formal political power in the hands of the central government, and despite the fact that one party, the Congress, has dominated Indian politics since independence – the party system has retained significant elements of decentralisation. The constituent states have consequently retained a wide influence over the administration of national policies.

Standing as they do at opposite ends of the spectrum of federal governments, the USA and the USSR clearly provide excellent examples of the diverse forms and guises that federalism has taken in the modern world. Moreover, the experiences of both states illustrate the point made earlier in the chapter that patterns and styles of centralisation and decentralisation in any state are liable to vary (often widely) over time. Thus, the present relationship – whilst still remaining identifiably 'federal' – between the national government in Washington DC and the fifty American states is clearly very different from the relationship between the national government and the thirteen original state governments agreed under the constitution of 1789. Similarly, the federal *structure* of government in the USSR – currently based on fifteen union republics – remains much the same as it was in the early 1920s when the present state emerged out of revolution and civil war. However, the *relationship* between the all-union (central) government and the constituent republics has varied over the years, albeit within much narrower limits than in the case of the USA.

Federalism in the USA

The political impetus towards the specific federal bargain agreed between the states at the Philadelphia Constitutional Convention of 1787, had emerged from the loose and unworkable alliance of these states under the Articles of Confederation. This bargain reflected the wish of the constituent states to surrender as little of their power as was possible, or was consistent with the establishment of an effective national government. Thus, under the constitution the federal government was given specific, but seemingly limited, powers over the clearly 'national' responsibilities of foreign affairs and defence, as well as a wider responsibility to promote the general welfare of the union by (among other less important duties) regulating commercial activities between the states and by providing a common currency. All other (undefined) political powers and responsibilities were to remain under the control of the individual states. Almost two centuries later this original conception of American federalism as a system of two autonomous levels of government with clearly divided authority, functions and powers has entirely disappeared. It has been replaced by a relationship without any clear division of powers between different levels of government, as the scope of government has increased. Today federal and state governments must co-operate and share growing responsibilities in accomplishing their joint tasks of governing the USA. In short, the complexities, as well as the costs, of making and implementing policies have ensured the blurring, if not the disappearance, of an originally clear distinction between national and state functions and responsibilities. Yet, at the same time, the original commitment to states' rights remains, in the form of strong and continuing support for the existence of two levels of government. It is also exhibited in the direct participation of the states in the composition of the US senate – two senators per state; in presidential elections – through the mechanism of the electoral college; and in the passage of constitutional amendments – which must be ratified by three-quarters of the states.

Although it remains a matter of dispute among scholars of American federalism when, and in what fields or areas of policy, the modern pattern of 'co-operative' federalism originally emerged, all are agreed that it had clearly triumphed by the twentieth century. In particular, the development in the late nineteenth-century of a system of 'grants-in-aid' ensured a much more homogeneous and closely-knit relationship. Through such financial aid the revenue available to the national government could be channelled to satisfy growing demands for more widespread and effective public services at state and local levels and to compensate for the wide variations of wealth among the states. During the present century this system of federal grant-giving has expanded enormously with the specific purpose of seeking to encourage the states to develop new social and economic programmes. Inevitably, this financial superiority has been accompanied by the imposition of national standards and guidelines and other conditions which the states must meet in order to receive federal funds. State and local governments are expected to carry out nationally-defined programmes, as well as to provide, within their budgets and resources, additional funds. However, national administrators also co-operate with their state counterparts in this implementation process, and, above all, seek to supervise and oversee the administration of national policies.

The Depression and economic crisis of the 1930s inevitably saw a major expansion and diversification of the grant system. The federal government expanded its aid to the often financially devastated states to enable them to develop more effective programmes in such vital areas as housing, social security and compensation for unemployment. Precise patterns of co-operation between the different levels of government varied from programme to programme. Further major developments in the federal pattern occurred in the 1960s, notably during the presidency of Lyndon Johnson, as the increasingly chronic state of decay exhibited by the largest and oldest cities in the USA created an acute urban crisis. This ensured that urban renewal became a major federal responsibility. A series of programmes in the field of urban development established direct links between the departments of the donor national administration and the recipient institutions and groups in the inner cities, often completely by-passing the traditional intermediary state-level organisations altogether. This system – which came to be termed 'creative' federalism – involved a departure from earlier conventions whereby the national government had channelled its finances through the states to lower levels. On the basis of a growing national concern over questions of civil rights and race relations, it also signalled an expansion of national governmental intervention into areas of policy – such as elementary and secondary education, electoral law and the design and establishment of electoral constituencies, as well as police powers and court procedures and standards – which had previously been left to state direction. The extent of this expansion in federal grant-giving is indicated by the overall figures for the years 1950 and 1969 – 2.2 thousand million and over 20 thousand million dollars respectively.

Nevertheless, with the benefit of hindsight it has now become clear that the 1960s marked the high tide to date of national governmental power and responsibility. Since then, despite a continuing rise (of about 10 per cent between the late 1960s and the late 1970s) in federal grants to state and local governments – which by the late 1970s covered nearly 28 per cent of state and local expenditures – the resultant ebb of responsibility and effective political power from the states to the national government has been substantially halted, and to some degree even reversed.

Politically, the election of a Republican president, Richard Nixon, in 1968, ended both a period of Democratic control of that office and the resultant rising tide of federal power and influence which had lasted (save for the interregnum of President Eisenhower between 1952 and 1960) since the 1930s. President Nixon and the Republican party were firmly committed to reduce the activities of the federal administration and to return power and resources to state and local governments. These developments in the 1970s, which came to be known as the 'New Federalism', resulted in the emergence of the block grant system of federal financing. Under this system states and local governments receive federal funds for some broadly-conceived purpose, and are able to then decide on the precise uses to which these funds are to be put.

The advent of President Reagan in 1980 reinforced this trend towards relying on block grants and the shift in the balance of control over specific programmes towards the states and localities. However, the main new factor in the federal balance over recent years has been the impact of economic recession and rising inflation on federal spending patterns and proposals. The emphasis is on cutting back overall federal expenditure. This, in turn, places an increasing burden on state and local governments which have already been adversely affected by the rising costs of inflation and unemployment and falling income and sales tax revenues. Significantly, city and local governments facing particularly severe local problems are increasingly competing with the states for available federal funds. Conversely, some states and regions are better able to cope with reduced funding than others.

Nevertheless, it is vital to stress that, if history is any guide, currently prevailing patterns in federal-state-local relations will change just as rapidly in the future as they have in the past in response to changing economic and political circumstances. Indeed, in the wider context of inevitable and continuing federal financial power, recent trends towards a greater decentralisation of control over spending from Washington to fifty states and to over 80,000 units of local government, are perhaps of relatively small importance for the long-term survival of the federal system. Much more vital is the existence and strength of a climate of public opinion (shared by political decision-makers at all levels) which recognises the historical and contemporary importance of regional differences in American society. It is this which supports a system of political institutions which was specifically designed to highlight and maintain the existence of these state-centred loyalties.

Historically, the existence of regionally and state-centred loyalties has been significant, not only for the development of American federalism but also for the development of the American party system during the nineteenth century. American parties have always been highly decentralised organisations compared to their British counterparts. This party decentralisation has both been encouraged by, and has in turn reinforced, the pattern of state-based politics imposed by the federal system. Thus, party organisation in the USA mirrors the pyramid of political institutions of the federal system, with separate and usually fiercely independent organisations existing at national, state and local levels. Consequently, federalism and the party system have each reinforced the impact of the other on the pattern of American politics, which, in comparison to most other contemporary states, remains remarkably decentralised.

Soviet federalism

Conversely, the example of the USSR provides classical evidence of the decisive impact of a highly centralised party system on a constitutionally and institutionally federal state. A policy of federalism for the USSR was initiated by Lenin and later implemented by the Bolsheviks after they had achieved power through revolution in 1917. This choice was a well-calculated political tactic in direct response to the multi-ethnic and multi-nation character of the Russian empire which the Bolsheviks sought to incorporate into the Soviet state. In so doing they correctly interpreted the mood of the non-Russian peoples of the former Russian empire. Their 'White Russian' opponents in the bitter civil war that followed the Revolution of 1917 blindly sought to base their appeal to the same peoples on an unthinking and unpopular policy of restoration of the pre-revolutionary and highly centralised imperial system. This initial successful tactical utilisation of federalism to tie more than a hundred nationalities together under Communist party rule, has in turn been repeated by Lenin's successors in the Soviet leadership. To date their policies have succeeded in making the USSR virtually unique among multi-national states in the quiescence of its ethnic groups. This quiescence is particularly notable since non-Russian nationalities now form about half of the Soviet population (47.6 per cent of the population in 1979), and are expected to be in a majority by the end of the current century.

The 1977 Soviet constitution claims that the USSR is a federal state, but one of a kind very different from the USA, since it is formed on the 'principle of socialist federalism'. The essence of this difference is encapsulated in Article 70 which describes the USSR as 'an integral, federal, multinational, state . . .'; a clause which one early Western translation interpreted as 'an unitary, federal, multinational state'! Quite explicitly, Soviet federalism, unlike its Western counterparts, claims to be compatible with a very high degree of political and administrative centralisation. This apparent attempt to combine opposites, is a basic necessity for a system of federal government which has an explicitly dual purpose. To quote Article 70 of the constitution again, the USSR claims to remain a 'voluntary association of equal Soviet Socialist Republics.' Yet it also seeks to draw 'all its nations and national-ities together for the purpose of jointly building Communism.' The first of these two very different objectives is in turn reflected in the institutional structure of Soviet federalism, which mirrors the multi-ethnic character of the USSR. The second is reflected in the manner in which the federal system operates, with a concentration of political and administrative decision-making in Moscow in an explicitly, and often rigidly, centralised manner.

Underlying the whole Soviet conception of federalism is the principle of *democratic centralism*. This theoretically involves the idea of a balance between central decision-making and local initiative. Although the precise nature of this balance has varied over the years, it has always remained very much tipped in favour of the decision-making power of the central authorities. Their principal consideration has been the development of the national economy through central planning. Thus, in practice, democratic centralism results in a clearly hierarchical system of decision-making in which there is an obligation on lower bodies to observe the decisions of higher ones. This, in turn, presupposes that on important questions such as those relating to the National Econ-omic Plan, the central government will have the final, and possibly only, say. Consequently, the powers granted to the federal government under the constitution (Articles 73 and 74) are unusually extensive compared to other federal constitutions. In particular, the financial and budgetary control of the central government is total. In complete contrast to Western-style federalisms, in which the autonomy of the different levels of government is buttressed by separate budgets, the USSR oper-ates with only one national budget.

Conversely, the powers of the fifteen union republics, which jointly comprise the Union of Soviet Socialist Republics, are correspondingly limited – despite the presence of article 72 of the constitution which promises that 'Each union republic shall retain the right freely to secede from the USSR.' Although this right to secession is often singled out by Soviet theorists as the most important characteristic of the Soviet conception of federalism, in practice it remains a right only as long as it is not exercised. The powers granted to the union republics at any one time are entirely dependent on the inclinations of the central, or to use the soviet term, the all-union government. The union republics have no inalienable rights. This subordination is explicitly sanctioned in the constitution. As Article 77 puts it, 'A union republic shall . . . facilitate exercise of the powers of the USSR on its territory, and implement the decisions of the highest bodies of state authority and administration of the USSR', – that is, the decisions of the all-union government.

The nature of federalism in the Soviet Union is determined by the requirements of a planned economy. The emphasis is on the strategic interests of the Soviet economy as a whole, and the union republics tend to be regarded as producers of specific commodities rather than as territories with independent needs. The essence of Soviet economic policy is that the economy of each union republic develops as a subordinate part of the single economy of the Soviet Union. As a result arbitrary changes have occurred within republics to meet central requirements. For example, Uzbekistan was changed during the 1930s from cereal to cotton growing, despite very considerable discontent based on the very reasonable premise that you could not eat cotton. Other equally arbitrary changes have occurred since, as for instance in 1963 when a cotton growing region in Kazakhstan was ceded to Uzbekistan. Similarly the boundary between the Russian and the Kazakh Union Republics was unilaterally altered by the central government in 1965.

Much vital administration must, of necessity, cut across the boundaries of union republics, which are, after all, based on ethnic and historical divisions. This gives rise to territories very unequal in size and resources. A brief glance at a map of the USSR shows the country dominated by the huge Russian

Figure 4.2   USSR: union republics

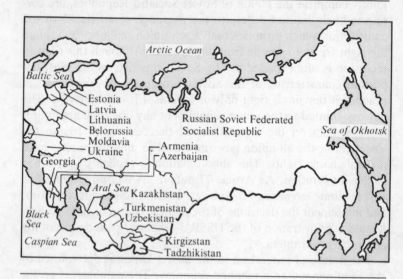

Republic with the other union republics clustered round the western and southern borders of the country (see Figure 4.2). Such arbitrary territorial divisions are inevitably inadequate as economic units for planning and industrial control. Although the federal structure provides for fifteen theoretically equal union republics, economic facts suggest a very different picture. Over half of the population of the USSR lives in one republic, the Russian. Perhaps even more importantly, two thirds of industrial workers live there, and many of the rest live in the neighbouring Ukraine. In this sense Russia dominates the Soviet Union economically, and together Russia and the Ukraine jointly dispose of the great bulk of the industrial wealth and might of the USSR.

Under Stalin, who dominated Soviet politics from the late 1920s until 1953, the independent powers of the republics were in fact almost non-existent. Industry was centralised under a system which basically by-passed the federal structure. The degree of centralisation in Soviet administration reached its peak in the early 1950s during Stalin's last years, while the disadvantages of this system became more and more obvious as the economy expanded. The centralisation of all control in Moscow gave rise to considerable administrative congestion and inefficiency as well as considerable dissatisfaction in the union republics. Indeed, the stereotypical picture of Soviet industry plagued by a succession of shortages and gluts had much truth about it. By the time that Stalin died the system of a centrally planned command economy, so efficient for rapid industrialisation, had in practice become an economic liability and required modification. Decentralisation was necessary, as the structure became incapable of coping with the tasks of control and supervision needed in an interdependent, advanced industrial society. This society posed problems too numerous and too technical for a monolithic administrative machine run almost entirely from Moscow. Flexibility was needed at all levels.

Nikita Khrushchev, who succeeded Stalin as party leader, constantly reiterated the irrationalities stemming from this Stalinist industrial system. One of his favourite stories was of building materials shipped from the western Soviet Union, near the Finnish border, to eastern Siberia whilst another Ministry had sent similar materials from Eastern Siberia to other parts of the Soviet Union. It was in response to muddles of this kind that Khrushchev implemented a policy of decentralisation. Hence, beginning in 1954, there has been a gradual extension of the powers and the responsibilities of the republic governments. Today union republic government is much more of a reality than it was in 1953, particularly over issues of cultural policy and other areas of purely or mainly local interest. The powers of these governments now even extend to such nationally important issues as economic planning, budgetary control and industrial management. However, especially in the economic planning field, all-union institutions ultimately remain supreme, determining budgets and allocating funds for capital investment projects. Conversely, republics may in practice still have their decisions countermanded by the central government. What has changed is that union republics now bargain with the central authorities on specific issues, most crucially over the availability of funds.

Decentralisation was not intended for the benefit of the republics or as a concession to the political aspirations of non-Russian nationalities, but rather to promote economic efficiency. Yet the process highlights an interesting paradox in that, over the three decades since the death of Stalin, the USSR has tended to become slightly more rather than less 'federal' in its governmental practices. In this sustained trend the Soviet Union is certainly unusual and perhaps unique among the governments in the world which would claim to be federal. The changes toward decentralisation may in practice be rather marginal, but they are interesting, and they have been sufficiently marked for the Soviet people, who are notably politically cynical, to joke about them. A typical example is the idea that, whereas Lenin originally provided democratic centralism and Stalin's rule brought bureaucratic centralism, the post-Stalin leadership has given the country bureaucratic decentralism.

Nevertheless, it must always be remembered that the most important political institution and the ultimate decider of all important questions of national policy, the Communist Party of the Soviet Union (CPSU), remains, as it has always been, a completely centralised organisation. In Soviet theory and practice federalism is appropriate only for the *state* not for the *party*. Party institutions stretch in a tentacular fashion from Moscow throughout the whole of the Soviet Union, and are regarded simply as the regional branches of a single hierarchical organisation. Furthermore, despite a theoretical commitment to an ethnically balanced party membership, the CPSU remains a thoroughly Russian-dominated institution. Thus, with 52.4 per cent of the population in 1979, Russians comprised 60 per cent of the party membership in 1981. Even more strikingly, the three Slav nationalities, the Russians, Ukrainians and Belorussians, whose share of the population – 72 per cent in 1979 – of the USSR is declining, collectively comprised 80 per cent of party membership.

**VERNON REGIONAL
JUNIOR COLLEGE LIBRARY**

5 Parties and Party Systems

Political parties: nature and impact

'The party,' argued Professor Samuel Huntington, 'is the distinctive institution of modern politics.'[1] In their present form – combining some degree of organisation and bureaucracy with some degree of mass membership and support – political parties are essentially modern structures. Parties have developed over the past two centuries to channel and to organise the mass political participation released by the gradual extension of the suffrage in emergent modern societies and states. Modern, organised political parties first appeared in the eighteenth century in the USA and spread from there to France after 1800. Both these states had the most widespread political participation and most generous suffrage at the time.

By the end of the century political parties had spread widely throughout the First World and beyond, gradually superceding and replacing the political cliques, factions, and family groupings which had dominated European and American politics in the eighteenth century. Like the factions from which they emerged, political parties are defined by their aim – the intention to exercise political power by placing their members in governmental offices – and by the methods that they utilise to realise this aim – their use of elections (as well as non-electoral methods) to place their representatives in office and to gain the widest possible degree of public support. Hence formal definitions of political parties tend to stress two features – election and office – and that offered by Professor Giovanni Sartori is typical. 'A party is any political group that presents at elections and is capable of placing through elections, candidates for public office.'[2]

Initially, the earliest modern political parties developed within representative and legislative bodies, and then developed 'outwards' into parties of mass representation. Later parties have

73

characteristically emerged to represent and press the claims to political representation and power of groups and classes hitherto excluded from such legislative bodies. This latter pattern has been followed equally by numerous European socialist and social-democratic parties, the ruling parties in the world's communist states, and most recently, by a multitude of nationalist parties seeking independence in the newest states of Asia and Africa. However, numerous modern equivalents of the former type of outwardly developing parties can be identified, most noticeably within the large group of military-dominated regimes in the contemporary Third World. In these states political leaders characteristically seek either to broaden their popular appeal or to civilianise their regimes by founding a political party. Equally, it must be emphasised that political parties in much of the contemporary Third World have a great deal in common with the cliques and factions of pre-democratic politics in the First World. Frequently such parties continue to lack both effective organisation and high levels of mass support. Thus, political parties in contemporary regimes are highly variable both in nature and in their origins, and this variability extends to their political significance and impact. While the explicit aim of the world's political parties is to control government, the extent to which such aims are realised is ultimately dependent on the extent to which parties are allowed or are able to dominate other political institutions – noteably bureaucracies, civil and military – which are also seeking to achieve or maintain political control. As Richard Rose stresses, 'one should conceive of the importance of party in government as a continuous variable rather than as an all-pervasive force; one can have more or one can have less of party government.'[3]

While organised political parties are widespread today, they are by no means ubiquitous features of political life in the world's regimes. Although more than one thousand organisations terming themselves political parties exist in contemporary regimes, a substantial number of states will, at any one time, be temporarily without parties and a small and dwindling group of states has never legalised them. By 1980 only ten of the world's states had never been ruled by a party government. This group of states continues to decline, slowly, in numbers, whereas the number of states temporarily without political parties has risen markedly over recent decades. Thus, in 1959, almost 80 per cent of the world's states were ruled by political parties of some sort. Then a decline set in during the 1960s and early 1970s, until, in 1977, only about 60 per cent of states had party governments. Since then numbers of party-dominated governments have increased again. However, the overall picture in the 1980s seems unlikely to deviate greatly from that in the 1960s and 1970s with, on average, over one-third of contemporary states without political parties at any one time – due mainly to the rapid spread of military rule in the Third World, a subject covered in full in Chapter 8. In 1980, among the 137 states independent for ten or more years, 93 (68 per cent) operated some form of party government. Moreover, party rule is far more obviously a feature of the First and Second World states than it is of the Third World. Of the 'Northern' states in these groupings only Greece, Portugal and Spain in the First World have not been under continuous party rule since 1945, and only Poland among the Second World states falls into this category. Significantly, by 1980 only one-third of Third World states had been continuously under party rule either since 1945 or since independence. Thus, the political party may be the characteristic institution of modern politics and the key institution in modern political systems, but it is also a highly vulnerable one, particularly in Third World states.[4]

Varieties of party system

The distinction made by the French political scientist Maurice Duverger over thirty years ago between one-party, two-party and multi-party systems remains the accepted basis for classifying party systems – that is the way party behaviour is likely to be influenced by the existence (or absence) of other parties. This classification – with the vitally important addition of no-party systems – also provides the most common basis for classifying regimes by identifying their predominant institutional patterns of government. The basic proposition remains, as Kay Lawson has pointed out, 'tell me how many parties you have, and I will tell you what kind of political system you have.'[5] Originally the rules of this 'numbers game' were very simple indeed. One-party rule and no electoral choice between competing parties meant that the system was dictatorial and authoritarian. Two parties made for stable democracy and the easy achievement of majority rule, with clear alternatives for the electorate to choose between. More than two parties led, at best, to rule by ineffective and transient coalitions and, at worst, to chronic political instability and the possibility of the complete breakdown of the system and the emergence of left or right wing dictatorship.

However, over recent decades these perspectives have been greatly modified as the sheer variety of different types of party system among contemporary regimes has become increasingly obvious. Specifically, it is now appreciated that one-party systems, although inherently authoritarian, vary widely and that, in particular, some are more genuinely representative of their populations than others. Equally, two-party systems may not always be so perfectly representative as earlier assumed, especially if faced by both a wide spread of political opinions from left to right and a diverse variety of hotly disputed political issues – for example regional or ethnic disputes as well as economic or class issues. Multi-party systems may in fact be highly stable, given the existence of long-standing coalitions between different parties sharing basic values. Thus, when considering the different types of party system currently in operation it is vital to remember that no one system is either inherently natural, or indeed best.

Although the first one-party state – Liberia in West Africa, governed continuously by the True Whig Party between 1877 and 1981 – emerged in the late nineteenth century, the phenomenon of the one-party state is pre-eminently a product of the revolutionary upheavals of the present century. In particular, the pre-revolutionary Bolshevik Party and the post-revolutionary CPSU provided a highly influential prototype and model. Currently one-party states are both numerous and widely distributed geographically. This situation underlines the point that this form of rule probably constitutes the most important single political invention of the twentieth century, and certainly merits its description as the principal modern form of authoritarian government. However, since this form of government occurs commonly among the economically and organisationally underdeveloped and unstable states of the Third World as well as in the more developed and stable group of states that constitute the Second World, many recent one-party states have been transitory phenomena.

Not surprisingly, the communist states of the Second World provide the majority of the twenty-five regimes that have been continuously ruled by a one-party regime since either the late 1940s or since independence. Similarly, the USSR is now the sole survivor of the original wave of one-party states founded in the years between the First and Second World Wars. Numerically, this group of one-party regimes was dominated by the Nazi and Fascist states of Europe. The Second World War destroyed the two prototypical examples of this latter group – Fascist Italy and Nazi Germany – but two one-party right wing dictatorships of this era – Portugal and Spain – survived into the 1970s. The spread of Marxist regimes following the Second World War, first in Europe and then in Asia, and, more recently in Latin America and Africa, had ensured that the bulk of contemporary one-party states espouse a left wing ideology. Nevertheless, the popularity of the one-party form among Third World states has ensured that this type of regime remains ideologically as well as geographically and organisationally diverse. Thus, of Third World states with uninterrupted records of one-party rule to mid-1984, Mexico, South Yemen, Tanzania and Tunisia, for example, are on the ideological left – albeit to varying degrees. Conversely, the Ivory Coast, Kenya, Malawi, Singapore and Taiwan are – again to varying degrees – on the ideological right.

Two-party systems – where parties are generally able to govern alone and some alternation in office occurs – although well-known as a category, are not very common. At the most generous estimate about twenty potential examples have existed over recent decades, with only about six relatively clear-cut cases – Australia, Austria, Britain, Canada, New Zealand and the USA. In fact – with the exception of the deviant case of Austria, a recent addition to the group – outside the English-speaking world, multi-party systems are as characteristic of First World states as one-party states are characteristic of the Second World. These multi-party systems typically possess oppositions rather than an Opposition, and the 'Westminster model' of government by a single majority party is replaced by a more complex system of alternative coalitions. Thus, governmental stability in multi-party states is crucially dependent not on the result of elections, but on the willingness of party leaders to negotiate and compromise in the aftermath of elections. Where the component parties and their leaders accept this need for negotiation and compromise to form governments, multi-party systems may well achieve stability – as in the contemporary cases of Denmark, Iceland, Luxembourg, the Netherlands, Switzerland and West Germany. Where all the important parties do not accept such a system of compromise – as in France until 1958, Weimar Germany, post-war Italy, and Spain between 1931 and 1936 – the result, at best, will be governmental instability. At worst, such systems, as in the cases of Spain and Weimar Germany, may collapse into dictatorships.

One type of party system fits only with difficulty into this basic threefold classification. This group of states is dominated by one party which, without coercion or fraud, persistently wins democratic elections in an otherwise multi-party system. Clearly, these states are not authoritarian one-party systems, since the winning party willingly surrenders power if and when defeated electorally. Equally, the number of states in this category depends on the strictness of the criteria used to define it, but long-term examples of this phenomenon are rather rare. Japan is a classic case, ruled by its Liberal-Democratic party continuously since 1955, as is India, governed continuously by the Congress party 1947–1977 and again since 1980. However, no other contemporary states have exhibited such long-standing democratic one-party predominance. All European examples of long-term one-party control – notably the Social Democratic parties of Ireland, Norway and Sweden – have seen significant periods of interruption to their predominance.

The development of party systems

Only detailed historical examination of the development of party systems in individual states will reveal exactly how and why that particular system developed in the way it did, and explain, in detail, all the variations among the individual political parties of which the system is composed. Moreover, it is now universally recognised that explanations of the development of particular party systems and the emergence of individual parties within these systems are enormously complex problems. This recognition of the complexity of causal factors contrasts markedly with the situation only a few decades ago when it was thought that party systems were primarily the product of the type of electoral system that was chosen. Although modern governments use a wide variety of different systems – the 1910 Report of the Royal Commission appointed to Enquire into Electoral Systems discovered over 300 different forms – all electoral systems can in practice be classified as variants of a small number of basic types. An electoral system is simply a method of translating votes cast by electors into seats in a legislature, and there are only three different ways that this allocation can be done – on the basis of a plurality of the vote, on obtaining the majority of the vote, or proportionately.[6]

Originally, it seemed that the impacts of these different types of system were clear-cut and unambiguous. Proportional representation, it was argued, led to multi-party systems, political extremism and unstable governments. Conversely the plurality system was said to result in two-party systems, political stability and the maintenance of democratic values. The evidence on which these propositions were based seemed clear since there exists a striking difference of geography and political tradition between states which adopted plurality systems and those employing proportional representation. Only Commonwealth states and the USA, following the British first-past-the-post model, have retained plurality systems of elections, and it is precisely these states which have provided the classical examples of stable two-party systems. Conversely, none of the states of continental Europe has adopted a plurality system; all have opted for various forms of proportionality (with the exception of France which, until 1985, had adopted a majority system). It was these states of continental Europe which provided the classical examples of multi-party government, chronic governmental instability and deep and irreconcilable ideological conflict.

However, further investigation of the relationship between party systems and electoral systems suggested that the earlier investigators had put the cart before the horse, and that electoral systems were not causes but consequences of different types of party system. Party systems in turn were themselves found to have been shaped by historical factors and social conditions and specifically by the number and type of divisions which emerged in a particular state. A large number of social divisions meant a multi-party system irrespective of the type of electoral system chosen. Thus, it became evident that proportional representation had been introduced into the states of continental Europe after, not before, the emergence of multi-party systems. This suggested that particular electoral systems are chosen because they suit the needs of the parties which exist and which naturally seek to entrench their positions. Moreover, it also became clear that the hypothesised impacts of the different electoral systems on numbers of political parties had been exaggerated: plurality systems do not necessarily reduce party numbers while proportional systems do not necessarily increase them. In particular, regionally concentrated parties – such as the Scottish National Party and the Ulster parties in the UK – gain more seats under first-past-the-post systems than they would under proportional representation. Indeed, mergers of parties and therefore reductions in party numbers have regularly occurred in states with proportional representation. In West Germany – where ten parties competed in the 1949 elections which inaugurated the Federal Republic – the imposition of a simple voting threshold (5 per cent of total votes cast) has ensured that only four political parties have been able to consistently achieve legislative representation at every election held since that date.

Even more importantly, it was discovered that multi-party systems fell into two very different groups according to both the numbers of parties and the nature and extent of the divisions between them. Proportional representation contributed to instability in the French Third and Fourth Republics and in Weimar Germany, and continues to contribute to governmental instability in Italy. It has clearly not encouraged instability in an even larger number of European states such as Denmark, Holland, Ireland, Norway, Sweden, Switzerland and West Germany. Indeed, in states such as Holland and Switzerland, proportional representation secures stability by guaranteeing representation to all significant religious or linguistic segments of often deeply divided populations. Overall, it became amply clear that the operation and impact of electoral systems is profoundly influenced by the political circumstances in individual states. 'The same electoral system', argues Vernon Bogdanor, 'can have quite dissimilar effects in different countries; or even in the same country at different period of its history.'[7] Above all it has become clear that the causal interactions and relationships between party systems, electoral systems and changes in societies are highly complex.

Parties: origins, organisation, ideology
Nevertheless, a limited number of generalisations about parties can safely be made, particularly in terms of their origins, their organisation, and their ideologies or political beliefs. Originally, the earliest modern political parties emerged from factions within legislative institutions, whereas more recently founded political parties have developed both inside and outside legislatures, not uncommonly as a splinter group from an existing party. Those parties that have been founded outside legislatures have origins that vary markedly from religious associations, youth societies and trade unions, to revolutionary movements. Invariably, the founding of a party is a conscious act undertaken by a relatively small group of key leaders who decide, rightly or wrongly, that an opportunity exists to place members of their organisations in positions of political power by winning popular approval. The impetus to undertake the necessary organisation and institution-alisation varies. It generally involves the occurrence of a political crisis which raises the political temperature and causes existing groups and factions to mobilise over issues of major political importance. Such crises might involve the extent of political participation allowed by ruling groups, or disputes over the territorial jurisdiction of the government and its attitude towards component regions, or over the legitimacy or moral right to rule of those in power. Organisationally, the élitism inherent in the origins of political parties tends to be perpetuated, and is often reinforced as the parties grow in size and organisation. 'Who says organisation says oligarchy,' wrote the German sociologist Robert Michels, referring specifically to the political party.[8] However, while all political parties are run by a relatively small number of individuals, the nature and extent of this control

Table 5.1   A typology of party organisation

Extent of membership participation	Dispersal of power	Centralisation of power
Active membership participates neither in policy-making nor in implementation of policy.	Committee	Cadre
Active membership participates in implementation of policy but not in policy-making.	Convocation	Vanguard
Active membership participates in both policy-making and implementation of policy.	Club	Mass

Source: adapted from Kay Lawson, *The Comparative Study of Political Parties* (St Martin's Press, 1976), p. 78, Table 3.2–1.

varies. Different parties allow different degrees of participation to their memberships. As Kay Lawson has suggested, three different questions are relevant here.[9] First, is power within the party concentrated or dispersed? Second, are members accorded any role in making party policy? Third, do members play a part in carrying out party decisions? Different answers to these three questions reveal six theoretically possible kinds of party organisation, to which the organisation of individual parties will roughly correspond. Relatively few parties will fit one type exactly. This organisational typology is set out in Table 5.1. For example, the two major British parties – both highly centralised organisations – are located between the cadre and mass types, with the Conservative party inclining more towards the former and the Labour party more towards the latter type of organisational model. Similarly, the two decentralised American political parties, the Democrats and the Republicans, are a blend of the committee and the convocation types. Equally, of course the same party can change over time from one organisational form to another. Currently, the CPSU – like other ruling communist parties – is clearly a vanguard party. However, this party was, for a good part of its earlier history, more clearly a cadre party.

Ideologically, parties are conventionally placed on a left-right spectrum, although very little work has been done to try and ascertain exactly what left-wing, right-wing and centre positions really entail. In particular, the term 'centrist' has been applied to widely different types of party – those whose stance falls between parties termed right and left, and those with conflicting and contradictory positions on different issues. It has also been applied to parties which appear to fit nowhere else because of their concentration on a single issue, as in the case of Farmers' parties in the Scandinavian states. Similarly, parties which might seem to occupy the political centre may, like the Democratic and Republican parties in the USA, be arbitrarily labelled left and right simply because one is slightly to the right of the other. Conversely, as in the British case, parties firmly labelled left and right can move, over relatively short periods of time, both towards and away from the ideological centre. Moreover such terms as 'radical' and 'conservative' vary widely in their meanings from one state to another. For example, the members of the British Communist Party would view themselves as radicals, if not revolutionaries, whereas members of the CPSU in the USSR may correctly be viewed as conservative in relation to the current social, economic and political system. Radicals in Second World states would, on the other hand, be those who seek to modify or abolish that system.

Parties also vary widely, according to the degree or extent to which they are ideologically committed. Ideology itself can be relatively unambiguously defined in relation to political parties – as, for example, in A.J. Milnor's contention that 'party ideology is an enduring set of principles related to a specific social group or interest . . . which apparently explains the past, understands the present, and predicts the future.'[10] On the basis of this definition, the ruling communist parties of the Second World are clearly ideological parties. Ruling parties in First World states, on the other hand, tend to pursue political issues with less ideological intensity, and Kay Lawson has suggested three further categories – issue-less, pragmatic and programmatic.[11] The issue-less party carefully avoids specific policy pronouncements and commitments altogether. The classical example of this type of party is provided by the French Gaullist party – particularly in the years following the foundation of the present Fifth Republic in 1958 when the party's sole and unabashed aim and *raison d'être* was to support the party leader, General de Gaulle. 'With de Gaulle, for France,' stated the posters, 'the Gaullism of the majority of the French, regularly shown by opinion polls and elections, relied above all on a simple belief in an exceptional man.'[12] Nevertheless, most First World ruling parties tend to fall into, or between, the two remaining categories – the pragmatic party dealing with problems as they arise, and the programmatic party with a long-range perspective which seeks to meet both current issues and achieve some future goals. Thus, British parties seem, on balance, closer to the latter type whilst American parties frequently appear closer to the former. However, as these examples highlight, parties vary markedly, and over relatively short spans of time, in the balance of their apparent interests – responding to the issues which force themselves onto the political agenda. Crises, for example, whether domestic or international, are hardly conducive to the balanced consideration of long-term aims.

The two case studies which follow – of the Soviet and American party systems respectively – provide excellent illustrations of major themes and variations among contemporary party systems and parties, in terms of number – one and two party respectively; origins – extra-parliamentary and parliamentary respectively; organisation – centralised and decentralised respectively; and ideology – ideological and programmatic/pragmatic respectively. Yet, at the same time, the studies also shed as much light on what is unique and peculiar to these states. Thus, it must once more be emphasised that, so far at least, studies of party systems have shown them to be particularly reluctant to produce 'generalisations which do justice to the historical experience of different countries.'[13] Indeed, this stricture proves its value immediately once the apparently obvious and incontrovertible contention that the USA possesses a competitive two-party system is subjected to more detailed scrutiny.

Parties in the USA

Historically, an examination of the development of American political parties since their foundation in the last years of the eighteenth century appears only to underline the point that two major parties have always dominated American politics. The Democratic party has had a continuous history since its organisation in Congress as a vehicle for supporting candidates seeking election to that institution during the presidency of Thomas Jefferson. It has been successively opposed by the Federalist, Whig and the Republican parties. Polling consistently over 90 per cent of the popular vote since the middle of the nineteenth century the Democrats and the Republicans have appeared to preside over a classically two-party system. Yet a closer examination reveals that the basic form of two-party competition is the surface expression of a very complex reality which in its diversity has many similarities to the workings of multi-party systems elsewhere.

If the ethnic, regional and social diversity and heterogeneity of American society is not fully reflected in party numbers it is more clearly expressed in party organisation. American political parties are, compared to their counterparts in most First World states, highly decentralised and lacking in effective national organisation. Although the two major American political parties possess an elaborate pyramidal organisational structure which is typical of political parties world-wide, this organisation exists more in theory than in practice. In particular, the national party organisations and the national party leaderships operate only every four years during presidential election campaigns. Even during these campaigns the control exercised by the national parties over state parties and, in turn, the latter's control over county and local organisations tends to be minimal. In particular, the national party organisations have no control over nominations for the national legislature. Nor have they any means of ensuring that party candidates – even presidential candidates – adhere to party policies either before or after they are elected. Thus, the decentralisation and absence of discipline which is so characteristic of the political parties in Congress (see Chapter 3) also pervades the parties outside those institutions. The local regional focus which is so characteristic of Congress is also reflected in the operation of the party system generally. In particular, the state and local parties which form the backbone of the American party system are, like congressmen, concerned mainly with local rather than national issues and elections.

Thus, the American party system can perhaps be more correctly viewed as one which is fragmented into fifty different party systems based on each individual state rather than as a truly national two-party system. This situation was particularly noticeable up to the mid 1970s since the divergence of many states from the national pattern of close two-party competition was often very marked historically. Historically about twelve states, concentrated in the South, were traditionally completely dominated by the Democratic Party. Similarly, up to the early 1950s, eighteen rural northern states were dominated, albeit to varying degrees, by the Republican party. Until the mid-1970s break-up of the 'solid' South, only about twenty states actually possessed truly competitive two-party systems. Such was the electoral imbalance overall, that for almost fifty years to 1980 it was suggested that a one-and-a-half party system was a more accurate description of the Democratic domination of Congress than the conventional two-party label. However, Republican organisation and electoral strength is now growing in the traditionally solidly Democratic South and the impact of this development, which has been reflected in presidential elections for over three decades, is increasingly felt in Congress. Thus, whilst the Republican party has won the presidency five times in the eight elections since 1952, the Democratic party controlled both Houses of Congress for all but four years between 1952 and 1980. Significantly, while the Democratic party has retained control of the House of Representatives into the 1980's, the Republicans achieved a majority in the Senate in 1980 and maintained their position in 1982 and 1984.

Moreover, as party behaviour within Congress underlines, there are almost as many disagreements and divisions within the two major parties as there are between them. To the observer, American political parties seem more like *ad hoc* coalitions of very different, sometimes even hostile and always discordant, groups or factions – historically most frequently regionally-based. These groups or factions come together rather infrequently to present a combined electoral platform which is then presented as party policy in presidential election years. Organisationally, the modern American party system dates from the election of

F. D. Roosevelt, a Democrat, in 1932, and from his attempts to counter the economic crisis triggered by the 1929 economic depression. Roosevelt built a Democratic electoral coalition composed of such disparate elements as the South, Catholics, Jews, Blacks, and trade unionists of the urban North. The basis of this coalition was the president's commitment to use the might of the federal government to rebuild the economy, provide employment and social services. Conversely, the Republican party was organisationally based on the rural and Protestant North. It built its coalition as the party of economc *laissez-faire* and of the free market, with a consistent opposition to federal regulation or the provision of further social services. The resultant absence of organisational coherence – best expressed in high degrees of factionalism and low voting cohesion in Congress – in the American parties is reinforced by the very low level of partisan involvement by the mass public. The idea of party membership has no real meaning or significance in the USA. 'In effect,' argues Hugh Bone, 'anyone who considers himself a Democrat is a Democrat; anyone who considers himself a Republican is a Republican.' As a result, suggests Clinton Rossiter, 'Even the loose-jointed Conservative and Labour parties of Britain look like armies of dedicated soldiers to the eye of an observer who has watched the ranks and files of the Republican and Democratic parties straggling across our political landscape.'[14]

Partisan involvement among the mass public has declined, as traditionally low levels of party identification and commitment have been reinforced in recent years by a striking loss of electoral support for the two major parties. In 1960, 63 per cent of the adult population voted in the presidential election. In 1980, only 53 per cent did so. 'Independents' – those who identify with neither the Republican nor the Democratic party – have formed 30 per cent of the American electorate since the mid-1970s. Interestingly, of the 70 per cent that continues to identify with one or other of the major parties those claiming to be Democrats continue to outnumber the Republicans by three to two. Yet, at the same time, it is clear that economic recession in the late 1970s under a Democratic president, Jimmy Carter, and a slow economic recovery under his successor, Republican Ronald Reagan, has seriously dented the 1930s image of the Republicans as the party of depression and the Democrats as the party of prosperity. The 1980 presidential election, in which Jimmy Carter, the incumbent president, only received 49 per cent of the popular vote, also saw a majority of all the ethnic and regional components of the Roosevelt coalition – except Blacks who remained loyal to the more activist party – desert the Democrats. Liberals and activists – those who support an active federal government – continue to gravitate to the Democratic party and conservatives continue to find their natural home in the Republican party. However, the election of President Reagan in 1980, and his re-election in 1984, on a markedly right-wing platform, suggested that a 'new right' coalition was possibly in the making. Reagan supporters, opinion pollsters discovered, consistently held a variety of conservative views which in previous elections would have seemed extreme, particularly when combined into a single platform. This platform argued that civil rights had been extended too far and too fast, that minorities and ethnic groups should practice self-help rather than seek government aid, that equal constitutional rights for women were unacceptable, as was abortion. Conversely, the platform maintained that moral and religious standards generally should be reinforced, not least in the nation's schools, that government activity should be reduced save in the field of defence, and most particularly so in the fields of environmental regulation, employment and living standards.

Apart from an increasingly volatile and unpredictable electorate, American political parties are now also facing a number of major challenges to their traditional function as organisers of elections – as a result of changes in campaigning style, campaigning finance and in the electoral role of the mass media. Since the late 1960s traditional party-based electoral campaigns have been increasingly replaced – for both presidential and congressional elections – by candidate-based campaigns featuring the individual politician rather than the party platform. These campaigns have attempted to appeal to the large numbers of electoral independents. Moreover, the organisational and financial basis of these campaign is less and less dependent on the party's resources and increasingly dependent on the efforts of the candidate and his own electoral team – who may or may not be supporters of the candidate's own party. The 1974 Federal

Campaign Reform Act – designed to clean up campaign finance in the aftermath of the unsavoury revelation of the involvement of members of Richard Nixon's Committee to Re-elect the President (CREEP) in the Watergate scandals – has placed ceilings on the money that can be obtained from private sources. It has also allocated almost all federal campaign contributions to candidates rather than to parties. Similarly, from the perspective of the candidate, television has become the main medium for the conduct of campaigns, while for the average voter television has become the most important source of campaign information. As a result, media specialists, advertising men and public relations consultants rather than party professionals have become key figures in individual campaigns. The candidate is 'marketed' and 'sold' – Joe McGinniss' *The Selling of the President* is the classic account[15] – like a commercial product. As a recent British textbook on American politics stresses, American political parties are 'in trouble'.[16] How deep this trouble really is can only be guessed at. Yet, such has been the historical adaptability and resilience of American political parties that their future, if uncertain and currently unpredictable, is not yet seriously in doubt.

The CPSU

It cannot be argued, in any sense, that the role of the CPSU in the Soviet political system is of declining significance. If anything, the reverse is true. Since the death of Stalin, the party has been increasingly recognised by Soviet and Western commentators alike as the most important of Soviet political institutions, and as a genuinely and permanently ruling party. Thus, a recent British text considers that the CPSU 'has strong claims for recognition as one of the most powerful political institutions in any country in the world.'[17] A Soviet political commentator has termed the whole Soviet political system a 'partocracy'.[18] Constitutionally, Article 6 makes the party's position crystal clear. 'The leading and guiding force of Soviet society and the nucleus of its political system . . . is the Communist Party of the Soviet Union.' Equally, if American political parties can be held to be among the most decentralised of political parties, it can also be claimed that the Communist Party of the Soviet Union – like its counterparts in other Second World states – is one of the most

Figure 5.1   CPSU organisation

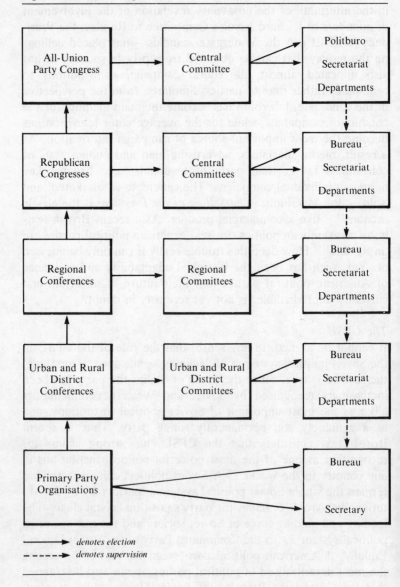

All-Union Party Congress → Central Committee → Politburo / Secretariat / Departments

Republican Congresses → Central Committees → Bureau / Secretariat / Departments

Regional Conferences → Regional Committees → Bureau / Secretariat / Departments

Urban and Rural District Conferences → Urban and Rural District Committees → Bureau / Secretariat / Departments

Primary Party Organisations → Bureau / Secretary

→ *denotes election*

----> *denotes supervision*

centralised parties in the world. This organisational centralisation is reinforced by an elaborate pyramidal organisational structure which, unlike its American counterparts, operates in practice as well as in theory (see Fig. 5.1). The CPSU projects party activity both regionally and functionally (within work-places) throughout the USSR in a manner that can best be described as tentacular. Similarly, and again in marked contrast to its American counterparts, the CPSU displays a very high degree of organisational coherence. It exhibits a party unity and an absence of factionalism – in public at least – which continues to border on the monolithic. Finally, CPSU organisation is characterised, once again unlike its American counterparts, by the strict standards of ideological and political commitment it requires from individuals to become and to remain party members. Underlying enforcing and explaining this high degree of organisational centralisation coherence and unity is the vitally important principle of democratic centralism.

Lenin, whose idea it was, contrasted democratic centralism with bureaucratic centralism on the one hand, and anarchism on the other. He stressed both the desirability of centralised control to secure discipline, and the need for democracy in order to secure the participation of all party members in party work. Subsequently, Soviet theorists have consistently maintained that the CPSU has operated according to these tenets. Nevertheless, even Soviet theorists appear to agree, at least implicitly, with Western analysts who have equally consistently pointed out that centralism has tended to predominate over democracy within the CPSU. A recurrent theme in recent Soviet writings on the subject has been the necessity to improve 'intra-party democracy' in order to ensure a genuinely two-way interchange between central and local institutions. In practice, it is clear that the four separate elements which comprise the doctrine of democratic centralism, as it is defined in CPSU Rule 19, are not equally applied. These elements are:

i) The election of all leading party institutions.

ii) Party institutions must make regular reports to superior institutions.

iii) Party discipline is strictly enforced, and the minority must totally accept the decision of the majority.

iv) The decisions of higher party bodies are binding on all lower bodies.

Clearly, the first element is the democratic facet, and it is this element which is least closely observed, in spirit if not in form. Conversely, the three other centralist elements are generally rigorously applied. In practice all 'leading party bodies' are indeed elected, but all elections above the level of the lowly primary party organisations (PPOs) are indirect. The greater the decision-making power of the party institution, the smaller will be the number of party members who are, even theoretically, able to influence its composition. Moreover, all party elections are closely monitored by 'higher bodies' and all candidates – through the operation of the system known as the *nomenklatura* – are in practice selected and approved by the central party apparatus.

It is vitally important to appreciate how comprehensive the *nomenklatura* system is, operating down to the level of chief agronomist on a collective farm, the head of a shop in a large factory, or the secretary of a PPO. All posts of responsibility throughout the USSR – some three million within the party alone – must have their occupants 'confirmed' by the party organisation at the appropriate level. At each of these levels the party organisation possesses a list (*nomenklatura*) of the posts over which it has the right of confirmation. The more important the post the higher up the party hierarchy the specific *nomenklatura* will be located. The most senior posts of all – some 300,000 – are in the hands of the party's Central Committee Secretariat. The institution controls all appointments to the highest posts in government (state) and party. In the latter institution it covers all posts in the Secretariat, the Politburo and the Central Committee and its apparatus, as well as the party secretaries and full-time party officials in the regions. Similarly top posts in the ministerial and soviet hierarchies are covered, as are senior positions in such vital institutions as the military and the secret police (KGB) as well as in the mass media and in public organisations such as the Komsomol – the party youth organisation – and the trade unions.

The party's claim from revolutionary days was to be an élite of the best citizens, and consequently it was never intended to be an organisation which sought maximal expansion. On the contrary, the party has always sought to recruit selectively, although from time to time there have been mass recruitment drives. Consequently, over its history the party has grown at a far from uniform rate and numbers in the party have in fact fluctuated very markedly over relatively short periods of time. Thus its composition was about 24,000 at the beginning of 1917, less than half a million at the time of the seizure of power in October 1917 and over 3.5 million by 1933. Membership however was down to just under 2 million in 1937, when a large number of members had been expelled from the party, imprisoned or shot on Stalin's orders, in what has come to be known as the Great Purge. By 1967 the party had 13 million members, by 1976 15.5 million, and in 1981 almost 17.5 million – an extremely large figure for a 'vanguard' party! Clearly with approximately one adult in ten a member, the CPSU is, in numerical terms at least, a genuinely mass party, and Soviet theorists envisage that membership will continue to expand. Analysis of the social composition of the party, even using Soviet data, suggests that despite the surface esteem for the working class in Soviet ideology, workers have in fact always taken second place to the white collar intelligentsia in actual party membership. The historical explanation for this is that the pre-revolutionary Bolshevik party was founded and led by, and indeed mainly composed of, intellectuals, and was a literate organ in a semi-literate society. This contrast persists, albeit in a modified form, today in that in particular the incidence of party membership rises very sharply as you move up the educational ladder. However, in the 1950s, Khrushchev shifted recruitment into the party in favour of workers, and this trend has continued under his successors. 1982 figures give the party's composition as 43.7 per cent industrial workers, 12.6 per cent agricultural workers and 43.7 per cent intelligentsia or white collar. Interestingly, the party remains male dominated, although the proportion of female members is rising steadily – from 19.7 per cent in 1957 to 27 per cent by 1982. Similarly, the ethnic composition of the party is uneven with the Russians, in particular, over-represented (60 per cent of party membership and only 50 per cent of the population). Despite constant efforts to build up party membership among non-Russian nationalities many of these are still under-represented and some, particularly the Muslim nationalities, are grossly so.

The core of the membership is composed of well paid, full-time officials, who staff the party *apparat* and are known as *apparatchiki* or *kadry* (cadres). The precise numbers of these functionaries, who have made a career of party work, is not known. It seems clear that their numbers have contracted since the 1950s, at least as a percentage of party membership. Following the death of Stalin there has been a drive to replace paid functionaries with volunteers. The best estimate appears to be that today approximately 100,000 or less party members can be viewed as party professionals. Better educated, on average, than the party's mass membership and considerably better educated than the average Soviet citizen, these *apparatchiki* have been described as 'the cream of the CPSU membership.'[19]

The party organisations with which the ordinary party member usually comes into contact – frequently described as the backbone of the party – are the primary party organisations (PPOs), which are formed in places of work and to which all party members must belong. Such organisations can be formed whenever there are three Communist party members, and it is party policy to form a primary organisation in every possible institution. Thus the number of PPOs tends to parallel growth rates in party membership generally. Accordingly we find 370,000 in 1971 and 419,670 in January 1982. These primaries have three broad duties: recruitment, educational work and the exercise of *kontrol* or supervision over their parent enterprises. Alongside this functional basis for party organisation – which dates from the conspiratorial pre-revolutionary days – the CPSU is also organised territorially. The territorial organisation of the party roughly parallels the administrative sub-divisions of the USSR with an all-union level and below this territorial party organisations in fourteen union republics stretching right down to urban and rural district organisations. Territorial organisation exists in only fourteen union republics simply because the Russion Union Republic has no party organisation separate from the national organisation centred on Moscow. This point underlines the fact that the union republic parties are not national parties but branches of a single organisation. Centralisation has always been a cardinal principle of party policy and any administrative decentralisation in the USSR must always be seen in the context of a completely centralised CPSU.

According to the party's rules, the All-Union Party Congress is the supreme party institution. At least formally, it is the job of the Congress to elect a Central Committee, which in turn, again formally, elects a Politburo and a Secretariat – a trio which together comprise the party's policy-making institutions. The party's Congress meets every five years with about 5,000 delegates attending. Given its size and infrequency of meeting the Congress is a highly formal institution without any pretence at policy making. It can best be described as a sounding board and a forum for the widest possible publicity for policies which have been decided elsewhere. The major functions of the Congress may be seen in terms of publicity and communication of policy plans, particularly to the delegates representing party organisations from throughout the Soviet Union, but also to Communist party members drawn from throughout the world.

Between Congresses, the party's Central Committee is theoretically the controlling institution, meeting at least twice a year, and often described as the party's parliament. This description is accurate at least in the sense that all major party decisions are issued under its authority – just as all laws in Britain are issued under the authority of parliament. In practice however, the policy-making powers of the Central Committee are rather weak. In particular, it is limited both by its size and by its infrequency of meeting. Central Committee plenums are regularly held immediately before important state and party events such as Supreme Soviet sessions and the announcement of new economic plans. They may also be called, on an irregular basis, to discuss specific major issues or problems such as the state of Soviet agriculture, or international tensions. The outcome is usually a decree which becomes binding party policy. Membership of the Central Committee numbered 470 in 1981, and its size grows as the party itself increases in membership. Nominally elected by the party Congress, the Central Committee is in fact selected by the top party leadership on the basis of some combination of personal merit and position occupied, and its membership follows a clear pattern. Its composition includes leading party officials from the national and regional party apparatus, national and regional government officials, and leading representatives of the military, police, trade unions and economic management, education, culture and science, as well as a token representation of workers and peasants. In practice it seems certain that the Central Committee is primarily a forum in which the top party leaders seek advice, information and support. This role could well be a very important one, since Central Committee members – representing as they do both the regions and key groups and institutions in Soviet society – are also closer to the day-to-day problems of administration than the top party leaders. It can therefore be assumed that the Central Committee may well be in a position to influence decision and policy-making.

The party's, and indeed the Soviet Union's, supreme policy-making organ, is the Politburo. Although theoretically elected by, and responsible to, the Central Committee, the Politburo is, in practice, like the British Cabinet to which it is often and reasonably compared, the real power centre which can, under normal circumstances, manipulate and control the Central Committee. The Politburo contains between twelve and fifteen full members, and with its candidate (non-voting) members totals up to two dozen in number. Like its British counterpart it is a highly secretive organisation and relatively little information exists concerning its operations. It is known, however, that the party general secretary leads and directs it, and that its membership includes all the most important political figures in the USSR. Furthermore, the outward features of the policy-making process have remained fairly constant in the years since the death of Stalin in 1953. For example, the Politburo meets once or twice a week – possibly more frequently during crises – to discuss major issues of policy and two former party leaders, Khrushchev and Brezhnev have told foreign correspondents how unanimity is sought via discussion.[20]

Whilst the Politburo is accepted as the major policy-making forum, the party's Secretariat plays crucial preparatory and administrative roles in the decision-making process. Under the party rules, the Secretariat has two specific functions. First it is given a responsibility for personnel selection – selection of cadres. Second, it is responsible for checking on the carrying out of party/state decisions, as well as a more vague responsibility for undertaking preparatory work for the party's formal decision-making bodies – the Central Committee and its Politburo. These seemingly quite mundane functions tend to belie this institution's very real political significance, although something of its importance may be understood by quoting Stalin, who was fond of saying, 'cadres decide everything.' The Secretariat can most appropriately be seen as the general planning and administrative staff of the party. It exists to provide the policy-makers in the Politburo with the necessary technical information and also serves to supervise the whole party apparatus and therefore, indirectly, the whole country. The Secretariat meets weekly under the party leader – the general secretary – and consists of about a dozen individuals of whom about half will also be Politburo members. Each secretary is responsible for a group of subjects which are administered through a number of departments, numbering at least twenty-three in 1980 with a permanent staff of thousands – estimates vary from a few thousand up to ten thousand. These departments parallel the subjects covered by the Council of Ministers and specifically oversee the activities and performance of the state ministries. Organised like a government in miniature and staffed by highly trained and skilled personnel, the Secretariat has been described as a Soviet version of the American White House staff, servicing both the general secretary and the Politburo.[21]

Parties in the Third World

In its structure and in its functioning the CPSU is no more – and no less – a political party than its less overtly ideological, loosely organised and highly decentralised, often weakly supported and only periodically governing, counterparts in the USA. From a global perspective, parties are clearly highly diverse and variable political institutions, and their diversity and variability is certainly not fully exhibited by the two national examples examined above. In particular, Third World parties and party systems differ markedly in practice – although often seeking to emulate in theory – from their counterparts in the First and Second Worlds. Often lacking both principal characteristics of the modern party – organisation and mass support – Third World political parties are not infrequently viewed as closer to the kaleidoscopic factions that formed, coalesced and disappeared around competing political leaders of the pre-democratic era, than truly 'modern' parties. At the very least, the transient nature and organisational weakness of most Third World parties – even in regions with long histories of independence such as South America – places them in a completely different category from their First and Second World counterparts. For example, the innumerable political parties which have appeared and disappeared in the Latin American states since their independence in the nineteenth century have given rise to the quip that to form a party all you needed was a president, a vice-president, a secretary-treasurer and a rubber stamp. If times were bad you could dispense with the vice-president and the secretary-treasurer!

Although there are notable exceptions – the Mexican PRI (Institutionalised Revolutionary Party) in power for over half a century and the Indian Congress Party, in office almost continuously since independence in 1947 – parties in many Third World states have remained institutions which are cynically utilised for the personal ambitions of individual politicians. They have been utilised by these individuals to build their own power on the basis of promises of the distribution of government jobs to loyal supporters. At its crudest in this system of 'patron-client' relationships, the patron – the party leader or notable – promises his clients among the voting public specific, often monetary, favours in return for votes. Alternatively, or in some cases, additionally, many ruling Third World parties, particularly in one-party states, are much more openly mechanisms of control through which the political leadership manipulates the mass of the population – either through overt coercion or through material inducements, or, more commonly, some combination of the two strategies. Only rarely are Third World electorates able to influence either the composition of the political élite or even its policies. Of the fifty-odd states which are members of the Organisation of African Unity (OAU) only one, Mauritius, has seen the party-composition of government change hands as a direct result of an election.

However, it must be stressed that neither patron–client relationships nor parties as mechanisms of élite control are unknown to contemporary First or Second World states – as the American 'spoils system', covered in Chapter 7 and the USSR's use of democratic centralism and the *nomenklatura* respectively underline. Where Third World parties do characteristically differ from their counterparts is in the narrowness of the élite group – sometimes even one individual and a very small number of his close supporters – which effectively operates, controls and benefits from the party system. Third World states also differ in the weakness, or absence, of mechanisms, both electoral and organisational, through which this élite can be called to account for its actions or inactions. Nevertheless, Third World parties, like their First and Second World counterparts, seek to perform the function of 'linkage'. All parties seek to act as 'intermediaries between citizen and state',[22] linking the public to governmental policy-makers, the ruled to the rulers. Equally it seems to be undeniable that, at least from the perspective of voters and rank-and-file members, many, perhaps most, of the world's political parties perform their 'linkage' functions rather less effectively than they could. In part at least, these failures explain why political parties are today increasingly challenged as governing institutions. Most spectacularly these challenges are posed by the powerful civilian and military bureaucracies discussed in Chapters 7 and 8. Less spectacularly, but no less seriously, parties, particularly in the advanced industrial states of the First World, are today challenged by pressure groups offering alternative forms of, and mechanisms for, the development of effective linkages between peoples and governments.

6 Pressure Groups in the Political Process

Group origins and forms: a classification

Political parties seek to integrate a number of the varied and different aims and expectations of their members and their voters into a comprehensive party platform. This is transformed, in part at least, into governmental policy once power is achieved. Pressure groups, on the other hand, tend to specialise in their aims, interests and causes, seeking to influence policies in only a limited manner and in a specific direction. Thus, while parties seek to undertake or at least to participate in the government of the country directly, pressure groups generally seek to influence, from outside, individual decisions made by the government. However, the division is not precise. Many pressure groups contest national elections, and, conversely, many political parties operate virtually as pressure groups. Moreover, in some states, certain important pressure groups have been incorporated into the governmental process to such an extent as to play, or appear to play, a role equal or even superior to that of political parties in the making of a very wide range of governmental policies. In theory, therefore, political parties and pressure groups offer overlapping but complementary forms of institutional 'linkage' between rulers and ruled, state and society. In practice the overlaps are obvious, but these two agents of 'linkage' may well be in competition for the ear of the government.

Pressure groups tend to be classified according to their differing origins and societal or institutional bases into three forms – communal, associational and institutional. These forms exist in varying permutations in different regimes, according to levels of socio-economic development, and according to the relative freedom allowed for group action. Communal groups are ascriptively based – that is, group membership is based on birth rather than choice – and involve a commitment to 'primary' ties based on a shared ethnicity, language, culture, or geography. Institutional pressure groups refer to the occupants of those political structures and institutions, notably bureaucracies and armies, which are in a key position to utilise their organisational strength. This enables them to pursue either the corporate interests of all their members or the narrower interests of smaller groups of their members. Finally, associational groups are those pressure groups deliberately and consciously formed and organised to achieve specific and limited aims for their members. Consequently such groups may either seek to promote a cause or an attitude, such as conservation or nuclear disarmament, or they may seek to protect a social or economic interest or section as in the case of trade unions and employers' associations.

Communal groups. The key distinguishing feature of communal groups is that they are an outgrowth of traditional forms of social and political organisation. Consequently, their numbers and their political importance are greatest in those societies in which these narrow, traditional loyalties continue to have a significance for daily social, economic and political life. Clearly, therefore, both the largest numbers and the most politically significant examples of communal pressure groups exist in the newly independent states of the South. Here the structures of modern politics and the institutions of the modern state are of relatively recent vintage and have frequently been grafted on to economic, social and political arrangements dating from an earlier pre-colonial period. In Africa, for example, ethnic, tribal and kinship associations and their offshoots in the form of local improvement associations and regional groupings, have, in the post-independence period, extended traditional African patterns of localised group organisation and action. These groups, responding to the new opportunities and threats presented by the modern state, have become increasingly politicised in defence of their members' interests.

It must be emphasised that such traditional communal pressure groups based on age-old ties are not necessarily to be regarded as of declining importance in modernising societies. Traditional cultures and traditional groups are frequently given unprecedented opportunities for expanding their impact through modern means of mass communication, such as newspapers and radio. Nevertheless, it is likely that in the long run, exclusively communal groups will gradually lose their significance in the Third World, just as they have lost their significance in the economically developed states of the West, and, as they are currently doing in the newly industrialising states of Latin America. In Europe a residue of earlier communal groups continues to exist in the form of broad social groups with a religious, class, linguistic, ethnic and regional basis. However, in order to maintain their political impact, communal groups have generally tended both to develop their organisation and to specialise their functions. From this process they have emerged either as fully fledged political parties, as in the case of working class socialist and social democratic parties and the Catholic-based parties of continental Europe. Alternatively they can become modern associational pressure groups, as in the case of trade unions, which, in the states of continental Europe, may equally have a Catholic or a working class basis. Thus while communal groups disappear, as such, communal underpinnings of associational groups remain.

Associational groups. Although associational pressure groups are an increasingly important feature in Third World regimes, most of these states, apart from those in Latin America, tend to lack powerful commercial and industrially based 'associations of associations' and 'peak associations'. Such groups, exemplified by the British TUC (Trades Union Congress) and CBI (Confederation of British Industry), exist in all the major industrialised and in some of the industrialising states of the world. These organisations, with their huge memberships and vast resources, are able to exert considerable and continual pressure on governments in a way that their smaller, more divided and less well-organised associational counterparts in the less developed states cannot hope to emulate. Moreover, those associational groups that do operate in the states of the Third World tend to be mainly of a 'protective' rather than of a 'promotional' type. Protective groups seek essentially to 'protect' the interests of their members – an aim which is perhaps best illustrated by the political activities of occupationally based groups such as employers' associations and trade unions. Characteristically, this political activity may take the form of specific demands for services or decisions perceived to be advantageous to the membership. Alternatively it may involve wider proposals for improvements in broader policy areas, for example calls for changes in economic policy. However, in both the states of the developed West and in the Third World, protective groups may well make wider efforts to influence the actual composition and personnel (and not merely the decisions) of the current political leadership. Indeed, this wider political involvement in questions vitally affecting the stability of particular regimes is actually more characteristic of Third World groups than their counterparts in the developed West, who can more safely leave the question of the actual composition of regimes to political parties and the ballot box. This characteristic Third World involvement in wider political questions may well not be confined to peaceful pressures, as the subversive activities of student groups and trade unions in the events which led up to the overthrow of the hereditary monarch in Ethiopia in 1974 powerfully underline.

Promotional groups, on the other hand, are particularly characteristic of the advanced industrial societies of the Western world. These are states in which the immediate issues of politics are not mainly those of life and death, starvation and hunger, and widespread and acute poverty, but also involve the distribution of an economic surplus, allowing a focus on the quality of life. In this context 'attitude' or 'cause' groups thrive, seeking to advocate or change policies on individual issues of topical concern, from abortion to vivisection. Since the aim of such promotional groups is not to defend the interests of an occupationally or communally defined segment, but to 'promote' their chosen cause, membership is typically open to all interested persons. Promotional groups, therefore, are the purest form of 'associational' pressure group, with their open membership and, usually, specific and limited aims. Typically the actively of associational groupings exhibits, over the years, a kaleidoscopic and ever-changing pattern. Organisations, like the currently ubiquitous ecology groups, will suddenly emerge in response to changing political issues and shifts in public opinion. Such groups may well, like the peace movements of the 1950s and 1960s, equally suddenly disappear from the political agenda and the public mind. Most of these groups will in fact disappear for ever, at least as political organisations, after their often brief, if sometimes spectacular, existence. Some, however, may hope for periodic resurrection – as, for example, in the contemporary case of the peace movements – when their *raison d'être* again becomes politically significant and publicly recognised.

The public and vocal activities of the innumerable promotional groups of contemporary Western states are absent in the Second, communist, World, with its restrictions on free and open discussion of issues. These states allow little or no scope for the free operation of promotional associational activities. This situation is exemplified by the persistent physical intimidation and legal harassment of the embryonic Soviet counterpart of the Western peace and anti-nuclear movements. Nor, indeed, do these states willingly tolerate those private and non-governmental protective associations characteristic of Western societies, as the fate of the independent 'Solidarity' Union under martial law in Poland starkly underlines. Ironically, pre-industrial, and therefore pre-communist communal groups, such as the Catholic Church in Poland and nationalist groups in Russia, have proved impossible to eradicate. Indeed they often retain an influence over populations which forces communist governments to make limited compromises to accommodate such pressures. This type of group influence is, in practice, more reminiscent of the Third than of the First World.

Institutional Groups. However, in most other respects the pattern of pressure group activity in the communist states of the Second World differs markedly from both the advanced industrial states of the First World and from that in the economically underdeveloped or industrialising states of the Third World. In these states institutional groups become, in the absence of any other formally organised pressure groups, of primary and often exclusive significance. In both the First and, particularly, the Third World 'institutional' pressure groups invariably have a major and sometimes -- under military and bureaucratic regimes – overwhelming impact on the making of public policy. Yet it is only in the Second World that pressure group activity takes such an overwhelmingly institutional form under all political circumstances and all regimes.

In fact Western notions of pressure groups and of the ways that they operate have only a limited relevance to the communist regimes of the Second World. In these states the associational and voluntary pressure groups of the Western world, which seek their own limited interests, are afforded no real legitimacy. For these are political systems which define their respective Communist parties as correctly and exclusively representing the interests of all sectors of society. Consequently, Western conceptions of 'pluralism' can only be applied to the potentially equally diverse and divided socialist states with major modifications. In pluralist theory pressure groups are viewed as the inevitable, spontaneous, and autonomous outcome of the legitimate divisions, diversities and conflicts within societies. Political activity, in turn, takes the form of open competition between these groups. The difference between the advanced industrial societies of the West and their counterparts in the East is that the divisions, diversities and conflicts in the former are expressed through autonomous and independent private groups. These divisions are mainly expressed in the latter states through group action *within* public or governmental organisations and institutions, since these are the channels within which political communication, discussion and debate are permitted. Consequently, group conflicts in the Soviet Union and other communist states tend to be expressed in struggles for influence *between* institutions and groups *within* the civilian and military bureaucracies and their ruling Communist parties. This predominantly 'institutional' basis for group action in Communist states is reinforced by the interestingly 'communal' character of employing institutions in such societies. In Soviet-type societies the employing institutions provide far more than mere salary, they also include numerous and important fringe benefits and perks. Over recent years, at least in the Soviet Union, income equality between comparable occupations has, broadly, been attained. Consequently these benefits – including housing, medical attention, schools and nursery facilities, as well as for some occupations, special shops – cover items of vital importance not only for welfare but also for privilege and social status. Since the quality, and to some extent the quantity, of these benefits will vary according to the political influence and success of the institution, the result is what has been aptly termed 'a fusion of institutional and individual interest not found in the West.'[1] For example, the politically powerful Soviet military has its own well-stocked department stores, and has funds available to assist officers in building country houses for summer vacations (*dachas*) or to holiday at the best resorts.

Pressure groups and the state: contemporary patterns of group activity and influence

Within any individual state, all groups will logically gravitate to those channels and will utilise those methods which seem likeliest to bring them closest to the decision-making process. However, both the channels and the methods which are available in practice will vary markedly from group to group, and may vary equally markedly from issue to issue and over time for the same group. Equally, in different regimes, seemingly rather similar groups clearly need to adapt both their channels of access to political decision-makers and the methods of pressure that they pursue. For all groups must conform to the institutional pattern existing and to the prevailing expectations about legitimate and allowable group behaviour in each individual state. Indeed, even within an individual state a change of regime may bring a marked change in institutional patterns and a corresponding change in group behaviour. For example, in France prior to the establishment of the Fifth Republic in 1958, groups concentrated their attention on a powerful parliament. Since 1958, pressure groups in France have progressively concentrated their attention on the increasingly powerful executive, tending to ignore a much-weakened parliament. Clearly, therefore, whilst the substance of pressure group activity may show an identifiable generic similarity among the diverse regimes of the contemporary world, the specific forms that it takes will vary markedly from state to state, and, over time, within individual states. To some extent at least, these variations underline the fact that pressure groups play, or are allowed to play, very different roles in First, Second and Third World regimes respectively. However, at the same time, it must also be emphasised that it is impossible to identify three clear and distinct patterns of group activity which correspond to this three-fold division of regimes. Different First World and Third World states, in particular, exhibit major variations in the nature, as well as in the importance and political impact of the group activity that they encourage or allow. Similarly, among the Second World states, even when the nature of group activity tends to be similar, the importance and impact of individual groups exhibit significant variations.

Monism and pluralism. In the first place, regimes differ widely in the encouragement they offer and the opportunities they present for independent pressure group activity. From this perspective a hypothetical continuum exists. On the one hand, there is a state of 'monism' – a complete absence due to state repression of independent group activity and the control of society by one single centre of state power. At the other end of the spectrum, there is a fully 'pluralist' system. This involves a state-encouraged equality of opportunity for the widest possible variety of independent and competitive group activity. It also requires the provision of a decision-making process which allows for equality of access for all these competing groups. This continuum can be depicted diagrammatically, with an assumption that any individual state can be located, roughly at least, upon it (Figure 6.1). However, it is important to stress that the two parameters of this continuum, monism and pluralism, are *hypothetical* end-points. Contemporary regimes cluster between them, with some falling closer to one end and some to the other. No contemporary regime (and no historical regime) has yet succeeded in abolishing group or factional activity entirely, although a number of regimes have successfully repressed and

Figure 6.1   Continuum of state encouragement/discouragement of independent pressure groups

Discouragement	Encouragement
Monism	Pluralism

outlawed organised and independent pressure groups. The most consistently successful regimes in the long-term repression of overt and independent group activity have been the socialist states of the Second World. Points similar to those made concerning the hypothetical nature of monism can also be made in relation to pluralism. No contemporary regimes do more than approximate to the criteria given above, with the politically competitive states of the First World most consistently coming closest to the pluralist ideal of equality of opportunity for all politically interested and active groups.

In the regimes of the Second World the Communist party has been presented as the sole, legitimate, representative political institution. All independent group activity has been actively discouraged and, if necessary, repressed – albeit to widely differing degrees and effects – if it has challenged this representational monopoly in any way. Moreover, as underlined in Chapter 5, ruling Communist parties have strict rules governing factionalism and group activity even within the party. These rules can be utilised, if and when party leaders wish, to strictly control the formation and operation of informal pressure groups within party-controlled political institutions – such as the institutional groupings in the USSR discussed earlier in this chapter. On the one hand, fully competitive group activity both outside and inside the confines of the Communist party remains theoretically unacceptable and ideologically illegitimate. On the other hand, the rulers of the individual socialist states are able to decide to what extent group activity can be tolerated or encouraged in practice. Consequently, the nature and level of group activity has differed very widely from one Second World state to another, as well as varying widely within individual states over relatively short periods of time.

From these perspectives, group activity among the European Communist states has clearly been highest in Poland, Hungary, Yugoslavia and, in 1968, in Czechoslovakia. In this last state group activity exploded suddenly in the 'Prague Spring' of 1968 when attempts were made to liberalise the regime. A similar rapid intensification of group activity occurred in Poland in 1980–1981 with the rise of the independent trade union 'Solidarity'. Robert Furtak divides these states into three categories on the basis of their attitudes towards group activity. The first category comprises the USSR, the German Democratic Republic, Czechoslovakia (to 1968), Rumania, Bulgaria and Albania. In these regimes party control over group activity remains very tight. 'Mass organisations', such as the trade unions and the party youth organisations, remain 'transmission belts' for the furtherance of party policy. The second category comprises Poland and Hungary where professional organisations of intellectuals, workers and of peasants have attained a certain degree of independence. Additionally, in Poland, the Roman Catholic Church has enjoyed a wide degree of independence from party control. Only Yugoslavia falls into the third category. With an industrial system based on workers' self-management, relatively independent trade unions, and different national republics competing for resources within a federal system, pressure group activity is often only loosely under the control of an often divided Communist party.[2]

Yugoslavia is also an exception in a further sense. For it, and Albania, are the only East European states which fall completely outside the USSR's sphere of political influence and military control. In all the other European communist states the negative attitude of the USSR to group activity has been, and remains, as crucial as the attitudes of national leaders. The invasion of Czechoslovakia in 1968 underlined the lengths to which the Soviet Union would go to enforce political conformity in Eastern Europe. The establishment of military rule in Poland in 1981, in turn, underlines the lengths to which national leaders in Eastern Europe are prepared to go to avoid this fate. Furthermore, as a result of the overpowering impact of the USSR, a setback to group activity in one East European state influences future trends in the others, either by discouraging further group activity in states like Hungary or by reinforcing the rigidly authoritarian and anti-group regimes such as the Rumanian.

The states of the Third World tend to cluster between the regimes of the Second and First Worlds in their attitudes to, and encouragement of, independent pressure group activity. In many Third World states, particularly those governed by military-bureaucratic regimes (see Chapters 7 and 8), attitudes towards pressure group activity are often thoroughly monistic. In these regimes the emphasis tends to be on creating an administrative or technocratic state run by the bureaucracy and somehow above 'divisive', 'inefficient', and 'parochial' party and pressure-group politics. However, since these states tend to lack the organisational and coercive resources available to Second World regimes, the outcome of many Third World attempts to repress or coercively to control group activity tend to be less uniformly successful.

Throughout the Third World pressure groups are increasing rapidly in number, if not always in importance. Conversely, however, the groups themselves tend to suffer from an endemic condition of organisational under development and low resources. Consequently, organised pressure group activity tends to remain weak in Third World States, despite the rising number of groups. These developments, moreover, continue to leave very substantial segments, and sometimes a majority, of the populations of Third World states outside formal group representation. In these states, low levels of education or the effects of geographical dispersion make group organisation difficult or impossible for significant segments. Even in Latin America, where groups are more extensively developed than in other Third World regions, the peasants or *campesinos* remain largely unorganised and politically weak and marginal. Throughout the Third World the growing numbers of the urban poor and unemployed also remain unorganised and politically ineffectual. Organised and effective Third World pressure groups, on the other hand, tend to represent the powerful and the wealthy, such as commercial and industrial interests and large landowners.

The states of the First World consistently allow and encourage open and independent political activity by organised pressure groups to a far greater extent than their Third World counterparts. Nevertheless, as in the Third World, some groups tend to be given a privileged consultative status as trusted 'insiders' – because of their organisational and financial power, or the extent of their popular support, or their importance to governments as providers of crucial information. Other groups, which lack these attributes, are not formally excluded from the consultative process. However, they often find in practice that a theoretical equality of opportunity for group activity is negated by inequality of access to crucial decision-making institutions. In particular, the states of the First World frequently tend to compound the problems resulting from the differential impact of individual groups. For group effectiveness is dependent not only on varying levels of human, monetary and informational resources but also on the extent of the concentration of decision-making powers in the hands of the executive. In executive-dominated states, such as the UK and other West European countries, the achievement of 'insider' status is crucial, since no effective appeal against executive decisions can be made by groups. In such states pressure on the legislature by groups means little more than a gesture of protest. Conversely, where, as in the USA, political decision-making is based on an inter-institutionally as well as an intra-institutionally competitive process crucially involving the legislature as well as a rather divided executive branch (see Chapters 2 and 3) the points of access for competing groups are increased. In these contexts, the advantages of 'insider' status are more limited. It is obvious, therefore, that the states of the First World differ in the extent to which they approximate to, or deviate from, a situation of genuine group pluralism. This point leads us to a consideration of a second criterion on which an evaluation of pressure group activity in different regimes can be based.

Pressure groups and policy-making. Those First and Third World states which allow open and overt pressure group activity differ widely in the influence over governmental decision-making – in terms both of the formulation and of the administration of policy – that they allow or offer to selected pressure groups. The key producer groups, both capital and labour, are rightly perceived to have a potentially major contribution to make to effective decision-making. In practice, however, regimes differ markedly in their attitudes to, and treatment of, such economically important groups. Again, this group-government relationship can be expressed diagrammatically (Figure 6.2). From this perspective, the low point of pressure group influence can be defined as authoritarian or state-enforced corporatism, and its high point as societal, liberal or bargained corporatism. Consequently any individual state which allows overt pressure group activity can be located, approximately at least, on this

Figure 6.2   Continuum of influence of major pressure groups over governmental decision-making

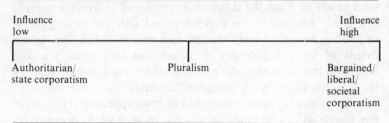

continuum. State or authoritarian corporatism occurs when pressure groups are 'licensed' by the state, which gives these 'corporate' groups a monopoly of representation in their field. In return for this official governmental recognition, the groups accept state control over their representational activities, and adjust their demands in line with official governmental policy. Under authoritarian corporatism pressure groups are entirely dependent on, rather than organisationally independent of, the government. Indeed their primary function is to exercise discipline on behalf of the government over their members' activities. Classically, as in Fascist Italy under Benito Mussolini, functional corporate groups, and particularly capital and labour, were formally incorporated into the institutional structure of the state to form *lo stato corporativo* – the corporatist state. Comparable systems of state-controlled corporatism operated, particularly in the inter-war years, in the other European Fascist or semi-Fascist states Portugal and Spain, as well as in Nazi Germany.

However, with the demise of European Fascism – in Italy and Germany as a result of the Second World War and in Portugal and Spain, in the 1970s, as a result of a military coup and of the dictator's death respectively – authoritarian corporatism is today most clearly characteristic of Latin American states. Significantly, these states were former Spanish or, in the case of Brazil, Portuguese colonies. Although the degree of governmental control over pressure group activity varies from one Latin American state to another, the usual situation is a much higher degree of state control than is characteristic of First World regimes.

Organisations such as the church, the university, the trade unions and the armed forces are viewed as part and parcel of a state into which they have been co-opted and absorbed by a theoretically mutually satisfactory bargain. Quiescence and support for state institutions and policies is given in return for some consideration of group aspirations and the formal recognition of the group's exclusive right to represent its particular sector or clientele. The alternative to co-optation and control through incorporation is repression, frequently directly by the armed forces, or with their approval. Co-optation is therefore an attractive alternative. It is a possibility offered to all Latin American pressure groups who can demonstrate that they have the support or political muscle to challenge or even overthrow governments if they are not co-opted and controlled. Originally, three groups provided the nine-teenth-century basis for Latin American corporate government, the military, the Roman Catholic Church, and large landowners. Often termed 'the nineteenth-century oligarchy' these core groups have now successively been joined, as economies and societies developed, by commercial élites, industrial élites, student and middle-class groups, and, most recently, by industrial trade unions and, in some states only, peasant organisations.[3]

At the other end of the continuum is the type of major econ-omic group-government relationship which, since the Second World War, has been increasingly common among First World states, particularly those in West Europe. This relationship has variously been termed societal, liberal or bargained corporatism. The importance of these developments can be judged by the fact that some academic analyses have suggested that pressure groups in certain of these regimes have now become more important than political parties as agents of 'linkage' between state and society, government and people. In systems of bargained corporatism, pressure groups, particularly major economic groups, have, as in authoritarian state corporatist systems, been semi-officially incor-porated into the governmental decision-making process.

However, the process of incorporation and its outcome have differed markedly from those in state-imposed authoritarian corporatist systems. Incorporation, in cases of bargained corpo-ratism, has been achieved on a voluntary basis as a result of bargaining and agreement between government and major groups. Pressures have come from the state and from governmental leaders to reduce wasteful competition between the major groups and the government. Likewise, it has been seen as desirable to encourage groups to involve themselves constructively in accepting responsibility for making and adhering to state economic policies and goals. However, these pressures from the state have been matched by equally strong pressures emanating from the societal sectors represented by the major economic pressure groups. The latter have sought to involve themselves and to influence governmental decision-making at the very highest possible levels.

Classically, the outcome of this process is that 'capital' and 'labour', in the form of the peak organisations representing the employers and the unions, operate alongside the elected government. The aim is a tripartite and co-operative or consensual system of governmental decision-making, particularly in the field of economic policy-making. Crucially, this system of inter-group and group-government co-operation and collaboration extends beyond the making of government policy to its implementation. The price the major economic groups pay for their privileged access to political decision-making as the reorganised negotiators for their economic sectors, is an acceptance of a very specific responsibility. They must ensure that their own members accept the resultant policies, even when these, as in the case of a price and wage freeze, are clearly unpopular with their members. Overall, this system of collaborative policy-making is frequently described by the French term *concertation*.

However, West European states in practice differ widely in the extent to which they approach this model of bargained corporatism; academics too have been unable to agree about the importance of these arrangements in individual states. For example, Switzerland has been described as both highly corporatist and a poor example of the system, while Britain, in the 1970s, has been described as both weakly and strongly corporatist. Nevertheless, despite these caveats, European states can be placed at least roughly on a simple scale of commitment to corporatist practices. Thus, in a recent essay Gerhard Lehmbruch defines Austria, the Netherlands and Sweden as strongly corporatist in their policy-making processes, whilst Denmark and West

Germany are defined as exhibiting a medium degree of corpo-ratism. Britain is also seen as falling into this intermediate category, although Lehmbruch places it close to the borderline of weakly corporatist systems such as France. In the former, both the CBI and the TUC are insufficiently centralised and hierar-chical in their control of employers and unions respectively to achieve the kind of control exhibited over their memberships reached in strongly corporatist states. In the latter, the possibility of group-government co-operation is undermined by the ideolog-ical divisions and organisational weakness of the trade unions and by the poorly organised and institutionally divided employers organisations.[4]

Moreover, as the British example richly underlines, the exist-ence and maintenance of corporate tripartism is dependent on the continued adherence of the parties involved to the implicit bargain on which such arrangements are based. Since 1979, and the election of a Conservative government uninterested in collab-orating with labour and capital in policy-making, tripartism has, if only temporarily, disappeared. Equally, the tripartite decision-making process of societal or bargained corporatism tends to fit the non-European First World states only very weakly, if at all. For example, in Japan the labour movement is politically weak and unimportant and the crucial working relationship is that which exists between business and government. The outcome has been described as 'corporatism without labour' with business groups, particularly big business, collaborating closely with the bureaucracy and the ruling Liberal Democratic party in the making of policy.[5] However, unlike the strongly corporatist states of Western Europe, business interests in Japan are highly competitive, and individual groups align themselves with the various competing factions which exist within the ruling party. As these factions jockey for political power, different business groups fall into and out of favour with the government.

Similar but stronger caveats must be made in relation to the USA where corporatist forms of pressure group-government relationships have tended to be strongly resisted and remain largely non-existent today. Policy-making in the USA, in a highly institutionally competitive political system with executive and legislature unusually well-matched in political impact, approximates to the mid-point of pluralism shown in Figure 6.2. In a pluralist policy-making process pressure groups bargain and exert influence from outside the governmental decision-making process. Implementation of policy is also undertaken by governmental institutions, and not by pressure groups. The autonomy of pressure groups to bargain and to exert pressure on behalf of their members in pluralist systems contrasts markedly to the restrictions on this autonomy – albeit of very different kinds – inherent in both authoritarian and bargained corporatist systems.

Nevertheless, all First World states, in their allowance of a wide range of independent group activity, approximate to a situation of group pluralism more closely than they do to one of monism. None has, however, achieved full pluralism. Some, like the USA, approach this position more closely than states which have been less resistant to corporatist and inegalitarian patterns of group activity. The USSR and other Second World states, on the other hand, in their active discouragement of independent group activity, approximate more closely than other contemporary regimes to a situation of monism. Third World states, in this, as in so many other fields of political activity discussed in this book, occupy intermediate positions on this spectrum of group encouragement and activity. Consequently, the case-studies of the USA and the USSR which follow provide interesting and contrasting examples of major variations in the nature and influence of groups among contemporary regimes.

Pressure groups in the USA: 'towards pluralism?'
The above quotation is taken from the title of the concluding chapter of Graham Wilson's excellent recent study of American pressure groups.[6] Pressure group activity in the USA does not, as yet, approach a condition of full pluralism, but the USA is still markedly more pluralist than most, perhaps all, other First World regimes. In particular, American pressure groups are highly visible and very numerous. The evidence from handbooks of trade associations and other sources suggests that by 1980 there were almost 15,000 such national groups and organisations. By 1977 1,800 organisations with over 40,000 employees were located in Washington. However, even these figures seriously underestimate both the sheer numbers of American pressure

groups and their variety. For they exclude both transient, single-issue groups and an increasingly significant category of group activity associated with the protection of the consumer and of the 'public interest'.

This variety is not yet, however, sufficiently great to define the USA as a fully or completely pluralist system. Many societal groups continue to be ineffectively represented. Specifically, E. E. Schattschneider has pointed out that 'the pluralist choir sang with an upper class accent,' and that representation of the most economically and socially deprived sectors of American society remained totally inadequate.[7] Additionally, in America, with a more purely competitive and market-oriented economy than most First World states, business has achieved and maintained a very high degree of political power and influence over policy-making without need to have recourse to overt political or pressure group activity. As Charles Lindblom has pointed out, in a competitive market economy public affairs will inevitably be dominated by two groups of leaders, government and business respectively. In order 'to make the system work government leadership must often defer to business leadership' he argues. In short, business occupies a 'privileged position' in the American political system and cannot simply be viewed as a pressure group like any other.[8] Consequently, although American trade unions have been, until relatively recently, far better politically organised than business, they have consistently fared much worse in terms of influence over government policy. Yet, despite these caveats, American society is becoming increasingly associationally rich, and the ever-growing numbers of pressure groups are today more active and better organised than ever before.

A number of explanations are conventionally offered for this plethora and variety of pressure groups. Americans, it is said, are 'joiners', and are more willing than citizens in other First World states to participate in group activity. Moreover, the impact of class on political behaviour is both more uncertain and more mild than it is in European states, and Americans, broadly, share a common political ideology. Even regional loyalties – historically so important in the American party and government system – appear to be of declining political significance. Consequently, it is suggested, divisions and disputes between pressure groups have, inevitably, become of major significance in American political life. Additionally, American political parties are not only decentralised but organisationally weak, and are becoming, seemingly, ever weaker as their public support and popularity declines. Their inefficiency as agencies of representation and 'linkage' – both as channels of citizen involvement in the political and governmental process and as responsive and responsible policy-making institutions – has, in turn, provided a representational gap into which their rival agencies of linkage, pressure groups, have stepped willingly. Finally, the institutional and institutionalised divisions between and within the separate branches of the American government – legislative, executive and judicial, as well as between its different levels, federal, state and local – provide unusually good and numerous opportunities for pressure group activity. In particular, the division of authority over the federal bureaucracy, between the presidency and a uniquely powerful legislature (explored in more detail in Chapter 7), ensures a much more open and competitive national decision-making process than in other, more executive-dominated, First World states. Non-governmental pressure groups thrive on this system of inter- and intra-institutional competition which allows them multiple points of access to governmental decision-making. Institutional and particularly inter-governmental pressure groups also thrive in a system in which the federal government provides finance for and regulates many state and local government activities. The 'inter-governmental lobby' representing state, city and local government units has now become one of the most important in Washington.

Thus, American pressure groups are highly conspicuous participants in policy-making in the USA. *Prima facie*, it would seem, pressure groups must be of unusually great political importance in that state. Yet, seemingly paradoxically, precisely the reverse is true, even in the case of the economically important 'interest' groups representing business, agriculture and labour. 'In many respects,' argues Graham Wilson, 'American interest groups look somewhat less impressive than many of their counterparts in Europe.'[9]

American pressure groups, in comparative terms, are organisationally weak. In the first place, the major producer groups

– business, agriculture and unions – represent smaller percentages of their potential memberships than their counterparts in Europe. Unions, for example, account for only 23 per cent of the total labour force in the USA, 40 per cent in the UK, 66 per cent in Austria and 80 per cent in Sweden. Moreover, of this 23 per cent only 75 per cent are affiliated to the major or peak organisation representing labour. Similarly, less than 35 per cent of American farmers are members of a professional association, and this represents a far lower 'density' of membership than that 68 per cent of potential membership achieved by one organisation, the National Farmers Union (NFU), in Britain.

As might be anticipated, America is bereft of powerful 'peak associations' comparable to the British TUC, CBI and NFU. The typical pattern is one of several competing groups within each economic sector. Farmers, for instance, are variously represented by the American Farm Bureau Federation, the Grange, the National Farmers' Organization, and the National Farmers' Union, as well as by large number of associations representing producers of specific commodities and crops. Frequently, these groups dispute bitterly over agriculture's political needs. Similarly, although American industrial unions have traditionally exhibited a higher level of political organisation than their counterparts in agriculture and business, their characteristic disunity as pressure groups is still very evident. Although much union 'lobbying' is channelled through the Washington organisation of the AFL–CIO (American Federation of Labor – Congress of Industrial Organizations), a number of the largest and most important unions are not members of this organisation. Moreover, left-right disputes between American unions are more widespread and serious than those among their British counterparts. Additionally, the former are frequently tainted with a reputation for gangsterism and corruption, which does little to help their social and political status. With the exception of the unions (in the form of the AFL–CIO), American pressure groups representing key economic sectors have also had a much less secure reputation for supplying reliable information on a non-partisan basis than their British counterparts. Similarly, due to their divisions and low membership, American pressure groups have not been noted for their ability to control the members of their economic sectors. Finally, the decentralised American governmental system influences the organisational strength and cohesion of pressure groups as well as that of political parties. Groups are, as a result, frequently federally structured, and state and local organisations may well operate independently, and sometimes in defiance of the national body.

Some individual pressure groups in America are, even in comparative terms, powerful – the oil companies and the defence industries are two frequently cited examples. However, pressure groups generally, and major economic groups in particular, play a considerably less important role in the policy-making process than their less conspicuous and publicly active counterparts in European systems. Fragmented and competitive governmental institutions may offer many points of access to groups, but the absence of any single decision-making centre makes the type of executive-insider group arrangements characteristic of Western Europe impossible. Americans generally, irrespective of political party affiliation, have been more hostile than Europeans to the adoption of economic policies, such as prices and incomes policies, which demanded co-operation between governments, business and labour. In recent years, the political tide has been particularly resistant to higher levels of taxation and to any extension of government negotiated or controlled economic activities. Equally, until very recently, business interests in general have found that successive American governments have been favourable to their needs and aspirations without any need for serious lobbying or for organised pressure group activity. Conversely, the traditionally higher overt degree of political organisation by American unions has been a sign of their industrial and political weakness rather than a proof of their power. Significantly, in Europe it was the emergence of powerful unions which encouraged the development of business organisations, and these developments in turn encouraged other social and economic groups to organise politically.

On the one hand, there are no signs that the prevalent social, economic and political circumstances, which have traditionally combined to keep American pressure groups relatively weak, are likely to alter in any fundamental way. On the other hand, there is no question that the pressure groups themselves have changed vastly in recent years. First, they are far more numerous; the 1960s and 1970s marked a veritable explosion in their numbers. Second, groups are more politically aware, more sophisticated in their techniques, and much better organised than they were twenty years ago. Third, group activity is far more comprehensive than it used to be, and now incorporates formerly excluded or under-represented population groups, such as women, blacks and Spanish-speaking Americans, as well as hitherto neglected causes such as animals and the unborn. Despite the large differences in the resources available to different groups, most causes and interests now have at least some representation. Unions and civil rights groups, for example, as well as a number of more specialised groups have taken up the causes of the traditionally grossly under-represented poor and elderly.

Above all, the traditionally equally neglected general or public interest has been taken up by a myriad of highly active, and often very effective, 'public interest' groups. These emerged, or, in many cases, re-emerged, in the late 1960s and the early 1970s to campaign either for causes such as environmental and consumer protection, or to pursue single issues such as abortion, most commonly from a right-wing perspective. 'Explanations of the rise of the public interest groups in the late 1960s will probably remain highly speculative,' argues Graham Wilson.[10] Affluence is one possible answer, encouraging or allowing Americans to take up issues concerned with the quality of life. Significantly, support from these groups has come disproportionately from higher income and professional sectors of the population. The widespread scepticism and loss of trust and confidence in American institutions and leaders in the 1960s – political, administrative, business and industrial – is another possible explanation. What is clear is that by the mid-1970s public interest groups had arrived in large numbers and had made a major impact both on the American political system and, in particular, on other (particularly business) pressure groups. Citizens' groups, espousing a cause or pursuing an issue without any occupational basis to their membership, made up 21 per cent of all groups represented in Washington by 1980 and half of these groups had been formed since 1960.

Common Cause, founded to press for honest and efficient

government and the best known of the new public interest groups, was launched as a mass membership organisation in 1970, and by 1974 had 325,000 members and a budget of $6.6 million. Consumer interests were most conspicuously represented by a number of groups run through Ralph Nader's Public Citizen Foundation and collectively known as 'Nader's Raiders'. Environmental protection groups also increased vastly in numbers and in popularity. The outcome of their collective efforts, even by the late 1970s, was considerable. Major successes included securing the reform of electoral and campaign law to reduce the possibility of corrupt financial practices, and forcing the enactment of legislation to protect both the consumer and the environment in numerous and important ways. However, many of these victories were won against very limited opposition from business interests, which remained politically unorganised and frequently inept, until forced out of their complacency by the very costly legislative successes won by the public interest groups.

It was the cost to industry and business imposed by the new consumer, and environmental laws and regulations which finally and for the first time forced American business to organise itself properly politically in the mid-1970s. Organisational and lobbying techniques pioneered by the unions and the public interest groups were increasingly adopted and refined by business and professional groups from 1974. Business lobbying in Washington increased markedly in its extent and in its professionalism, with the number of corporation lobbyists rising from 8,000 in 1974 to 15,000 in 1978. Older 'peak organisations' of businessmen and industrialists, in particular the Chamber of Commerce, have reformed and reorganised to become more politically active and effective. Additionally a new organisation was formed in 1972 specifically to represent large corporations, the Business Roundtable. The Roundtable has rapidly become a very important pressure group, with particularly good links to the executive branch of government as well as to Congress. It specialises in the provision of accurate technical information, and in utilising its members' expertise in an essentially non-partisan manner comparable to many European employers' organisations. As a result of these reforms and developments, business had restored its political pre-eminence by the late 1970s, despite increasing co-ordination and co-operation between public interest groups and the trade unions.

Nevertheless, in order to regain its political influence, the business world has, for the first time, 'been forced to play pluralist politics,'[11] and forced to openly mobilise its enormous financial power for political purposes. In turn, its political task has been eased by the changed political climate since the late 1970s. In a context of fear over continued economic prosperity as unemployment rose, and of worries over the impact of inflation and world recession on incomes, the costs of the goals of the public interest groups have become more and more obvious. At the same time the importance of continued business confidence for future prosperity has become equally self-evident to a majority of Americans. Yet the public interest groups and their causes have only lost ground. These groups have not disappeared, and they remain an important goad to both businessmen and politicians.

Finally, American pressure groups have been quick to take advantage of the declining importance of political parties in the electoral process, and of the increasing fluidity of American voting patterns. Until the 1970s, the trade unions were the only economic sector which consistently attempted to influence elections. Since changes in campaign finance legislation in 1972, other pressure groups, particularly business interests, have sought to influence candidates by providing campaign donations through PACs (Political Action Committees). By 1978 business was supplying 15 per cent of total campaign funds, approximately the same amount as contributed by the unions. Indeed, if the contributions of business groups are added to those of their political allies, such as the American Medical Association (AMA), business-oriented interests now outspend unions by a majority of two to one at elections. Overall, therefore, it seems clear that American pressure groups, now overtly rather than covertly dominated by business groups, have become more effective organisations for political representation and 'linkage' than ever before. Nevertheless their impact on policy-making shows no signs of achieving European levels of significance.

'Imperfect monism': the USSR and pressure groups

The activities and importance of the major governmentally-based 'institutional' pressure groups in the Soviet policy-making process inevitably raise the question as to whether that state possesses or allows pressure group politics in the Western sense. Soviet ministries and other Soviet governmental or state institutions compete, like Western ministries and institutions, for scarce financial and other resources. Unlike their Western counterparts, however, their influence is, at least theoretically, more heavily constrained by the very tight control exerted by the CPSU over the policy-making process. Moreover, on close examination an institutional pressure group such as the Soviet military is perhaps more accurately seen as a number of different, and sometimes competing pressure groups. Sometimes these are based on clear-cut organisational divisions, such as inter-service rivalries, and sometimes based on more personal links, such as those binding the members of the 'Stalingrad group' (i.e. those who participated in the battle for Stalingrad in 1942). This group remains an influential personal network at the summit of both the military and the ruling Communist party. Soviet administrative agencies are technically obliged to take an overtly 'party' approach to decision-making and to renounce narrow departmental interests in favour of the wider interests of the nation as a whole. 'Nevertheless,' argues Jerry Hough, 'it is abundantly clear that Soviet administrators continually fall into the trap of "departmentalism".'[12] The prevalence and importance of 'narrow departmentalism' (to use the Soviet term), in addition to the persistent 'localism' discussed in Chapter 4, in turn underlines the importance of inter-institutional competition in the Soviet governmental process. This competition between different institutions and levels of government has been variously termed 'institutional pluralism', 'bureaucratic pluralism', 'centralized pluralism', and 'institutionalized pluralism'.[13] Leaving aside (to the final, concluding chapter of this book) the question whether the Soviet Union can correctly be described as pluralist in this, or indeed in any genuine sense, this type of depiction of the Soviet political system also suffers from a further major difficulty. For disputes between governmental departments and institutions over scarce resources and institutional competition are, to some degree, a universal characteristic; the USSR's experiences with 'depart-mentalism' and 'localism' seem mild in comparison to many other states. Indeed, the term 'institutional pluralism' is a particularly apt characterisation of the government of the USA, with its extreme fragmentation of political and governmental power and highly institutionalised system of inter- and intra-branch compe-tition. However, it is precisely the lack of the kind of 'stiffening element', exemplified by the CPSU, to enforce centralised disci-pline on the governmental process which makes the USA 'the system of "institutional pluralism" *par excellence*'.[14] Conversely, the overwhelming impact of the CPSU makes the USSR a rather poor candidate for this particular description.

The autonomy of Soviet institutional pressure groups to pursue their own perceived interests is therefore limited. This lack of autonomy has, in turn, encouraged other specialists in the study of Soviet politics to view group activity in the USSR as a species of corporatism. For corporatism, in both its variants, implies the existence of forms of pressure group activity without the necessity for any 'pluralist' assumptions about competition between auton-omous and independent groupings. Since the degree of discour-agement of group activity, both within and outside ruling Communist parties, varies from regime to regime in Eastern Europe, it is not inconceivable that forms of authoritarian or state-sponsored corporatism will soon emerge in Yugoslavia and perhaps in Hungary. However, this development assumes the open encouragement and sponsoring or licensing of non-governmental group organisations and activities to an extent to which the rigidly centralised and party-monopolised USSR does not even approximate. As long as non-party 'state' and 'mass' organisations like trade unions remain mainly 'transmission belts' for the furtherance of party policies, and as long as the party controls the selection of their leaders – through the *nomenklatura* process described in Chapter 5 – 'it will be premature to see the Soviet Union as an example of a corporatist state'.[15]

How, therefore, can we best describe the distinctive charac-teristics of the group activity that clearly exists and is as clearly tolerated in the USSR? First, it is an activity which occurs within institutions, but one in which group interests tend to be based as much on loose and informal groupings with common or shared attitudes and wishes as on the formal organisations themselves. These loose and informal entities, operating within or between formal organisations, are perhaps best described as 'opinion groupings', since they exist within broader occupational or professional categories, and may actually cut across occupational and institutional lines. Their existence has been increasingly recognised and allowed for by Soviet theorists in the post-Stalin period. Thus, one Soviet scholar, B.M. Lazarev, has argued that administrative personnel have 'personal and group interests which can foster or hinder the appropriate fulfilment of this or that function or competence.'[16]

It is now accepted that a complex modern society like the USSR inevitably contains a great variety of specific personal and group interests. Provided individuals and groups share the underlying common aim of building a communist society, these secondary and subordinate interests are deemed legitimate by the CPSU. Political, and particularly party institutions, are therefore expected to respond to these individual and group views and to take them into account when making policy, lest an absence of attention and a failure to consider all shades of opinion leads to the aggravation of disputes and disagreements. Thus, Lazarev has described the task of the party as bringing these legitimate conflicting interests into harmony, and to ensure the priority of 'integral interests' over departmental ones, and of the interests of the state as a whole over local interests. This writer openly discusses the policy-making importance of 'the conflicts between the general interests of the state as a whole' and the interests of different levels and branches of government, as well as referring to personal and group interests and conflicts within and between these organisations.[17]

The type of group activities and conflicts that the Soviet system engenders and allows have, in turn, been highlighted by a number of case studies undertaken by Western specialists. For example, Donald R. Kelley examined environmental policy-making and the specific question of pollution control in Lake Baikal in Siberia. His researches revealed three separate categories of groups. First, an industrial-commercial lobby, based on government ministries. Second, a state environmental protection lobby, again based on government ministries and agencies. Third, quasi-official conservation organisations allied with informal coalitions of environmentalists, collectively forming an environmental 'opinion group'. His conclusion was that the *ad hoc* and informal environmental lobby, in alliance with the state environmental protection agencies, played a key role in achieving more effective protection for Lake Baikal.[18] Other case studies have highlighted the operation of the 'personal interests' described by Soviet scholars, particularly in the form the increasingly important policy-making role played by technical and scientific specialists. Non-governmental specialists, often drawn from academic life, have been found to have participated increasingly in policy-making, alongside political leaders and institutional groupings, since the death of Stalin.

Nonetheless, despite a general recognition of the growing significance of group activity in the USSR, accounts generally agree that the groups which have so far emerged are not and cannot be Western-style pressure groups. For these groups are not free to pursue whatever interests they represent or whatever causes they wish to espouse. For example, another Soviet scholar, G. Shakhanzarov, has underlined that legitimate interests are not those 'narrow, parochial interests' which would involve 'a distortion of the principles of planned management of the national economy' and may 'seriously harm the common cause.'[19] Ultimately, the CPSU retains firm control over the question as to which particular interests and groups will be deemed legitimate at any time or for any specific issue. Significantly, when 'dissent' or 'dissidence' emerged in the Soviet Union in the mid-1960s – in the form of movements or groups seeking to pursue independent cultural and scholarly activities, to defend civil and human rights, and to press for religious freedom and national rights – the response of the authorities was harsh and immediate. In the mid-1980s, still struggling to organise and to exist despite constant police harrassment, these genuinely nongovernmental groups, as Gordon Skilling stresses, do 'approximate in some ways interest associations in democratic societies.' Above all, the activity of organised groups of dissidents as well as those of individuals like Solzhenitsyn or the Sakharovs – whether undertaken for religious, national, or more narrowly political purposes – 'represents a genuine pluralism of ideas and opinions, expressed openly, without censorship . . .' Nevertheless, these ideas and opinions can only appear in *samizdat* (underground) writings, which are privately and secretly printed and copied, and surreptitiously circulated.

These dissenters and dissenting groups operate only at the very margin of the Soviet political process, and their numbers are, in relation to the total population, very small. As a result, their direct impact on Soviet politics is also very limited. Yet, at the same time, their indirect significance is very great, not least because the hostile and violent reaction of the USSR to 'dissidence', both at home and in Czechoslovakia and Poland, tells us a great deal about the realities of Soviet power. This power remains concentrated firmly in the hands of the CPSU, and this, in turn, makes the USSR 'essentially monist' rather than either corporatist or pluralist. Consequently, Archie Brown has recently suggested that the terms 'diversity within monism' (paraphrasing a Soviet scholar's own description), or 'imperfect monism' (ressurecting Gordon Skilling's discarded term), are 'probably less misleading' than other descriptions of the Soviet system.[21]

7 Contemporary Civilian Bureaucracies

Bureaucracy: nature and impact

Civilian bureaucracies and their military counterparts – aptly termed the 'armed bureaucrats' by Edward Feit[1] – are ubiquitous political phenomena. Civilian bureaucracies occur, without exception, in all contemporary regimes. Moreover these civilian bureaucracies remain in the modern world – as they were in the historic empires and kingdoms of China, Egypt, Rome and Byzantium – institutions of central political importance. Indeed their political influence and impact has, if anything, increased in the twentieth century, as their functions and responsibilities together with their numbers have expanded in the present era of 'big government', managed economies and welfare states. Professor Jean Blondel argues that future historians will surely describe the current century as 'the age of bureaucracy'.[2] Not only has there been an enormous growth of governments, both central and local, but the public sector has also expanded beyond the traditional remits of governments to include innumerable commercial and industrial enterprises. Consequently, public sector employment has increased very markedly.

This trend is common in both the First and the Third World, and is inherent in the socialist Second. In Britain in 1977 21.3 per cent of total employment lay in the public sector. The comparable figure for the USA was 17.2 per cent while that for Sweden had reached 27.5 per cent. The 1851 census shows that there were 75,000 public employees in the UK. By 1979, the total number employed in the UK public sector was almost 7.5 million. In the USA the federal government alone employed a civilian work-force of over 3 million by 1980. However, among Western states France now has the largest public sector, arising from the programme of nationalisation undertaken by the socialist government in 1981–82. After this nationalisation the state's share of French industry had risen from 18 per cent to 32 per cent and its share of GDP rose from 33 per cent in 1960 to 43 per cent in 1981.

In the newly independent states of the Third World the expansion of the state sector has been even more dramatic and spectacular. Thus, in Africa the government has become the largest single employer in the modern sector of the economy. Characteristically, this public sector has become vast relative to other sectors of generally weak, agriculturally based, economies. Post-independence Africanisation of colonial bureaucracies has not only resulted in an indigenisation of personnel but also in an enormous expansion in the number of central government departments and governmentally-based public enterprises. In 1958 – before independence in most African states – it has been estimated that there was a total of 100,000 European civil servants in the whole continent, and these expatriates occupied almost all significant civil service posts. In 1975 one country, Nigeria, dismissed 110,000 civil servants from its vast and inefficient bureaucracy. Although reliable statistics for public sector employment are hard to find for many African states, the small Southern African country of Lesotho is probably not unrepresentative with 25 per cent of modern sector employment to be found in the public service. Nor is the comparable figure for Kenya of 40 per cent of all recorded employment unusually high even for an African capitalist state. Even more striking is the situation in the avowedly socialist or Marxist states of Africa with their explicit adoption of central planning, a command economy and an extended public sector. For example, in the tiny socialist state of Guinea-Bissau in West Africa out of a total of 24,000 regularly employed persons 15,000 belong to the bureaucracy!

It should not be assumed that rapid bureaucratic growth and very large public sectors are only characteristic of the newly independent or poorest states of the Third World. In the well-established and comparatively economically developed states of Latin America large and growing public bureaucracies are equally common. Even in these states 30–50 per cent of the gainfully employed labour force is in government employment and 40–60 per cent of GNP is generated by this public sector. Growth rates in public employment can be equally spectacular in this region, particularly in states and at times when the rates of growth in the private economic sector are low and government agencies are compelled to absorb at least some of the excess labour supply. Thus in Chile, which until a bloody military coup in 1973, had been one of the most stable and democratic of Latin American states, total population rose by about 24 per cent between 1940 and 1955, while the national bureaucracy increased by 60 per cent.

However, it is in the sixteen states that currently form the core of the communist Second World that this expansion of bureaucracy has reached its apogee. Here the public sector has expanded to such an extent that the idea of a private sector becomes more or less meaningless. The range of institutions, like the press, the trade unions and cultural bodies, which in the First World remain outside the state sector, are firmly incorporated under political control in a unified and centralised system. In these states the communist parties, through a strict control of appointments to all significant posts, oversee the operations of all economic, political and social organisations. 'The point,' argues Professor Alec Nove, 'is that in spite of formal distinctions between party, governmental, social and cultural organisations there is an important sense in which all are part of one great single hierarchy.' Within this hierarchy the ruling party controls all appointments of any significance. This system, appropriately, has been described as 'bureaucracy writ large'.[3]

Bureaucracies in contemporary regimes tend to share a common characteristic – professionalism. This has given these institutions in the modern world, as in the ancient world, great political advantages, leading in some cases to direct political power. Bureaucratic service is, in most contemporary states, a professional career frequently giving security of tenure. This situation of permanence and fixity contrasts markedly to the relative impermanence and transience of political leadership. It allows the bureaucracy to accumulate experience, technical information and specialised skills which transient politicians may well be unable to cope with or combat. With these advantages provided by their permanence, contemporary bureaucrats – both civilian and military – are potentially in a position to compete with the other institutions of central government and to expand their influence over the making and implementation of policy, unless their power and autonomy is firmly checked and controlled. Thus, in theory there exists a common assumption that bureaucracies should function as servant rather than master, and, in particular, that a distinction should be made between the making of policy – the prerogative of the political leadership – and administration or execution – the function of the bureaucracy. In practice, this seemingly straightforward distinction remains impossible to sustain since every problem, however technical, raises issues of political significance, and every decision, however insignificant, involves an element of political choice. Inevitably, this situation undermines any attempt to draw any sharp or absolute distinctions between the roles of politicians and bureaucrats. Consequently, the problem for all regimes becomes not one of whether the bureaucracy has political functions and hence political influence, but how many political functions it has, of what kind and to what extent.

Controlling bureaucracies: professionalism and politicisation

The influential political functions inevitably undertaken by professional bureaucracies has inevitably led to a concern by governments in all types of contemporary states to discover ways of counteracting the institutional advantages held by bureaucrats, and to establish secure means for maintaining political controls over them. Significantly, the two main methods utilised to secure political control over bureaucracies are similar, whether that bureaucracy is civilian or military. Indeed, there are powerful arguments for considering armed forces simply as a form of bureaucracy, albeit with guns, and, as the next chapter will argue, for considering military rule as a specific form of bureaucratic government. Nevertheless, the very special position occupied by the military in all contemporary regimes – due to their possession of a practical monopoly of armed force, as well as their important symbolic status as the defenders and guarantors of the state's independence – also grants armed forces a potential political significance and importance that civilian bureaucrats cannot hope to match – an ability to take control of government by force. Accordingly the two bureaucracies will be dealt with in separate chapters, and the remainder of this chapter will be concerned exclusively with civilian bureaucracies, or, to use the British term, civil services.

Paradoxically, one of the methods utilised by contemporary regimes to counteract, or to avoid, what might be viewed as excessive bureaucratic influence in the political process, is to utilise and manipulate the very resource that forms the basis of bureaucratic influence in the first place – their professionalism. This approach seeks to define bureaucratic professionalism in terms of subordination to political control and to establish a professional ethic among bureaucrats that equates profession- alism with service to, rather than control over, amateur politi- cians. In effect, this method of control views the solution as 'internal' to the bureaucracy, in that it seeks to develop a situ- ation under which the bureaucracy is self-policing. This method places the onus on the bureaucrats themselves to develop and to enforce, through their systems of recruitment, training and promotion, a specific view of the bureaucrat's proper role *vis à vis* politicians. This hoped-for view is one of political impartiality or neutrality towards contending political parties and ideologies, and one of loyal service to the government of the day, irrespec- tive of its political beliefs.

The second method utilised by contemporary regimes to secure bureaucratic subordination to political control – control by poli- ticians – is to deliberately politicise the bureaucracy. By means of the judicious use and manipulation of recruitment, education, training and promotion this method of control seeks to imbue bureaucracies with overt and explicit commitments to the political goals of the government of the day. This approach is primarily 'external' in its emphasis, in that it sees the government of the day actively involving itself in establishing and enforcing among bureaucrats those political standards and beliefs which it seeks to encourage. Conversely, this method of control also involves ruling groups in actively eradicating beliefs which they regard as inimical to their political goals.

In practice, all contemporary regimes utilise a combination of both professional (internal) and political (external) controls to ensure that their public bureaucracies remain politically account- able, although the specific emphasis chosen may vary very widely. In general terms, the competitive liberal-democratic regimes of the First World tend to emphasise, in theory at least, the primary importance of internal professional controls. At the same time, they have reinforced these controls by varying forms of external oversight, and, in most cases, by some deliberate politicisation of at least the highest echelons of the civil service. Conversely, the politically centralised socialist regimes of the Second World rely primarily on a very high degree of politicisation among their bureaucrats to ensure their loyalty and responsiveness to political direction. Only secondarily do they rely on internal standards and a professional ethic of obedience to politicians. Third World states, while usually possessing formal Western-type bureaucratic structures as a result of colonial rule, have tended to opt increasingly for overtly political controls over their civil services. This trend towards external control has been notable both in avowedly socialist states of the Third World as well as in those which have adopted a capitalist economy.

First World bureaucracies

These different emphases in patterns of control over the bureaucracy are, in turn, explicable in terms of the very different historical experiences, political ideologies and attitudes, of these three groups of states. In the Western liberal-democracies, traditions of bureaucratic service to the state frequently go back over centuries, and the expectation of their total loyalty to the state is therefore deeply entrenched. Characteristically, the most senior civil servants in such states are accorded a high social status and considerable prestige. They are intimately involved in the making of decisions on matters of high policy and form a small cohesive group of 'notables'. In return they accept some restrictions on their overt political activities while they remain full-time civil servants. The nature of these restrictions varies from state to state. For example, in West Germany civil servants are denied the right to strike, whilst much more comprehensive prohibitions against overt political activities exist in Britain.

Moreover, a strong *esprit de corps* is engendered by the existence of a small, powerful and prestigious élite group or – to use the now outmoded British term – 'administrative class', usually no larger than one to two per cent of the total civil service. This is frequently reinforced by the social and educational homogeneity of those who are recruited to these positions. Thus, an analysis of the class backgrounds of senior civil servants in eleven Western states revealed that the highest proportion of civil servants of working class origin was 21 per cent.[4] Significantly, this percentage was recorded for the USA where public service is accorded lower prestige than a business or legal career, and where competition for posts in the higher civil service is less keen than in states such as Britain, France and West Germany. This situation reflects the fact that recruitment based on merit criteria inevitably favours candidates of middle-class origin who, as a result of home background and education, are more likely to possess the intellectual and social skills needed to succeed in a highly competitive entrance procedure. Furthermore, recruits to such posts also tend to come from remarkably similar educational backgrounds, as, for example, in the admittedly rather extreme case of Britain, where almost two-thirds of senior administrators come from two universities, Oxford and Cambridge.

Interestingly, there are greater variations among Western civil services in terms of types of education required for recruitment than in terms of level of education needed. In fact, among Western states at least three different emphases exist, each with different educational requirements corresponding to a different conception of the task of the administrator. The first type is exemplified by the United Kingdom with its 'generalist' view of administration, where the emphasis is on a non-specialist educational background favouring those who have received a traditional liberal education in the arts and humanities. Here the view has traditionally been one of training 'on the job' with trainee administrators expected to pick up the art – not the science! – of administration as they move from one civil service department to another in their early, apprenticeship years. The second type is typical of continental European states such as Austria, West Germany and the Scandinavian countries; here, a legal background is preferred for general administration and between 50 and 70 per cent of higher civil servants have had a legal training. The remainder also tend to possess some form of 'professional' qualification in fields such as education, engineering or medicine. Furthermore, these European states also tend to follow recruitment by a further extended period of specialised academic training rather than relying mainly on simple 'on the job' instruction. The French example is notable with administrators trained at two famous and highly prestigious 'schools', the Ecole Nationale d'Administration (ENA) for general administrators, and the Ecole Polytechnique for specialists. Moreover, graduates from the latter then frequently proceed to further specialist schools covering such highly specific topics as mining, highway and military engineering. The third pattern is typified by the USA where a remarkably high percentage (about 40 per cent) of administrators are recruited from among natural scientists and engineers. This emphasis reflects the American preference for recruitment to specific administrative programmes with their attendant requirements for specialised technical expertise. This situation contrasts markedly to the British approach of recruiting a 'generalist' whose specialism will become administration itself.

However, whatever the variations exhibited by differing patterns of recruitment and training among Western bureaucracies they tend to share in a common heritage. This allows them considerable leeway and autonomy, frequently developed over centuries, over the internal structure and management of the civil service. Over the years, such bureaucracies tend to have won wide responsibilities for supervising the overall conduct of their own service and over specific matters of corporate concern such as recruitment, training, promotion, remuneration, personnel management and general conditions of service. In states such as France which in the past have suffered from chronic political instability – where, it was said, Republics and governments may come and go while the administration remains – bureaucracies became largely self-regulating out of neccessity. In France, sixteen constitutions in less than two centuries and the constant fall of governments prior to 1958 thrust an enormous political burden on the administration to maintain the continuity of government. In return the bureaucracy won, to a large degree, the ability to police themselves through their willingness to identify with whatever regime was in power at the time, and to serve it well.

Nevertheless, despite the characteristic autonomy won by the bureaucracies in First World states, governments in these systems have sought to reinforce and to secure internal controls through the enforcement of external political controls. The rationale for this process is a simple one. Internal control is desirable but insufficient for, as Herman Finer succinctly suggested, 'to rely on a man's conscience is to rely on his accomplice.'[5] The authority to control the structure of bureaucracies, and to reorganise their constituent units – usually ministries or departments – lies, as might be expected, in the hands of the political executive in both presidential and in parliamentary systems. Again however, as might also be expected, the USA stands apart from the majority of First World states as a result of its uniquely powerful legislature. In that state the decision to sanction executive reorganisation has traditionally rested with Congress. Significantly, however, since 1949 Congress has allowed presidents to propose administrative reforms including the creation and abolition of executive departments, but has reserved the right to review and veto these proposals if it disapproves.

In most First World states, executive control over bureaucratic structures is supplemented by some form of legislative supervision of the operations of the bureaucracy. Typically, these are centred, as in Britain, on a system of specialised committees. The US Congress, with its extremely powerful committee system, provides a unique example of a consistently effective and powerful system of legislative supervision. This system is based on the power to control the funds that the departments of the American Federal Bureaucracy seek. Consequently, the impact of the hearings of the various congressional committees – which probe the activities of the departments and scrutinise their estimates, frequently calling senior civil servants to provide personal evidence – are ultimately based on budgetary powers and sanctions. These powers and sanctions enable the American Congress to directly enforce responsibility for maladministration in a way and to a degree that is not open to most First World legislatures. Most of these legislatures, like the British parliament, are under executive control through the enforcement of more or less strict party discipline. However, in all First World legislatures the activities of individual MPs offer an additional instrument of redress for bureaucratic wrongs suffered by their constituents. In the USA, this activity is an important part of what is known as 'constituency service', while in Ireland it has been more bluntly described as 'going around persecuting civil servants.'[6]

In some First World states, such as Britain, legislative supervision is further hampered by long historical traditions of governmental privacy and secrecy. In this context the British experience contrasts markedly with that of the USA and Canada – which over recent years, and in response to growing public distrust of governments, have passed a number of 'sunshine laws' providing the public access to bureaucratic records and meetings and allowing them much greater freedom of information. It also constrasts with that of the Scandinavian states, notably Sweden. In the latter country public officials have been referred to as working within a 'goldfish bowl' due to the virtually complete system of public inspection and governmental openness that operates.[7] This system allows not only individual but also press access to information that would be securely classified in Britain. Thus, in First World states with long-standing traditions of administrative secrecy, such as France and West Germany, a much greater onus falls on non-governmental (but not apolitical) bodies such as the press and pressure groups to ensure that both internal and external political and governmental controls over bureaucrats are firmly maintained and enforced.

The experience of both the USA and Sweden suggests that the achievement of more 'open' government, of greater freedom of information and the enforcement of public accountability of officials, is perhaps as much or even more a matter of will and commitment among both public and government as it is a matter of institutional mechanisms. This partly explains why that Scandinavian invention, the ombudsman, – an independent official with the specific task of investigating complaints against administrators – has seldom been as effective as in its native Scandinavia, although it has been widely copied by other First World states, such as Britain (where a Parliamentary Commissioner for Administration has operated since 1967). New Zealand, Israel, Japan, France, West Germany (for military affairs) as well as by several of the states in the USA. At the same time, limitations on the global effectiveness of ombudsmen also owe much to deliberate institutional restrictions on their powers to investigate. For example, the British parliamentary commissioner requires

a request from an MP before investigating a complaint of maladministration or administrative abuse of power. Similarly, the
French Mediator's Office can only be described as a pale imita-
tion of the Scandinavian ombudsman, who, unlike these West
European counterparts, has complete independence of initiative.

Consideration of the ombudsman – a quasi-judicial institution
– leads logically to a consideration of legal checks on bureaucracies, which although present in virtually all contemporary regimes
may, superficially at least, take very different forms. In
particular, states vary in the extent to which they allow their citizens to challenge the activities of bureaucrats either through
special and separate administrative courts or alternatively
through their regular legal structures and court systems. In practice, however, the distinctions between states which have established separate systems of administrative courts and of
administrative law, and those which have not formally done so,
tends to be less than absolute. Among First World states the
distinction tends to be one of degree. States which utilise the
conventional court system for administrative cases, such as
Britain and its former colonies, including the USA, as well as
Denmark and Norway, have also developed within their bureaucracies large numbers of specifically administrative tribunals.
These tribunals have their own separate structures and legal standards and deal both with matters of purely administrative relevance, such as taxation, as well as with growing numbers of legal
complaints against specific bureaucratic acts.

However, there remains a clear distinction between these
states and states such as France, West Germany and Sweden
which utilise administrative courts to deal with all legal questions
affecting the administration, rather than allowing important legal-
administrative disputes to reach the regular courts of law. For
states with such separate systems of administrative law, the
French example has proved seminal with its network of administrative courts and tribunals established within the administration and culminating in the *Conseil d'Etat* (Council of State).
These courts are, however, staffed by judges who are either
former administrators themselves or were at least trained as
administrators. Consequently, whilst their activities are clearly
feared by administrators, such courts are to be seen as an internal

rather than an external form of control. Thus, it has been suggested that French administrative courts are both slow and timid in investigating politically sensitive issues. The Court of Accounts, for example, has the task of investigating financial irregularities. After belatedly adding its criticism of a series of recent and very public financial scandals involving government departments, it has been described as being 'like the army of Offenbach, [since] its courage was restored when it was clear that it could reach the battlefield only after the battle was over.'[8] Similarly, the Council of State, the ultimate court of appeal against alleged administrative abuses, not only operates with a several year backlog of cases, but has one third of its decisions ignored by the responsible officials. The relative ease of access to a separate system of administrative courts must therefore be balanced against problems arising from any mainly internal control mechanism – *quis custodiet ipnon custodes*? who guards the guardians?

Overall, what must be emphasised is the inevitably rather limited nature of available internal controls over powerful bureaucracies. A similar point must be made about the equally limited nature of the external controls that generally rather weak legislatures and vastly more powerful, but also vastly outnumbered, political executives can operate, at least on a day-to-day basis. Consequently it is not surprising that politicians in First World states have tended to utilise varying forms of politicisation of the higher bureaucracy to ensure its compliance. The executives in First World states have consistently sought varying degrees and types of power over senior bureaucratic personnel, ranging from the ability to move civil servants from one post to another, to the ability to appoint and remove bureaucrats according to their political commitments and suitability. In contemporary Britain, successive Labour and Conservative governments have consistently complained that the civil service is unwilling to throw its full weight behind economic, political, or social reforms of a fundamental or of a radical nature. These complaints have led to a series of hitherto somewhat piecemeal measures to enhance political responsiveness and to increase external political control.

These measures have stopped firmly short of any direct or explicit policy or political appointments within the senior echelons of the departments of government. However, informally at least, Britain appears to be moving in the direction of states such as France and West Germany where there is a clear convention of moving civil servants whose sympathies lie with the party in power into positions of political sensitivity as well as of administrative importance. Such a tendency has also been prevalent in other First World states where one party has either dominated the government over a long period – as in the case of the Japanese Liberal-Democratic party – or where – as in the case of the Italian Christian Democrats – one party has predominated over a long period in changing coalition governments. In these states, politically motivated promotions and demotions are considered normal, and significant sections of the bureaucracy have become colonised by these electorally dominant political parties. Civil servants are therefore forced to recognise and respond to the realities of political power.

The strict rules operating in Britain effectively forbidding any overt political activity on the part of career bureaucrats are not operative in most other First World states. In states as varied as France, West Germany, Greece, Japan and Sweden it has not been unusual over recent decades for over one-third of both legislature and government to be composed of career civil servants. This has resulted in a fusion of bureaucratic and political leadership quite different from the strict separation still prevailing in Britain. In France this overt politicisation of the civil service has meant that one interesting institutional innovation, *cabinets ministeriels*, or ministers' private staffs have, over recent years, become staffed almost exclusively by regular civil servants, albeit politically sympathetic ones; their functions have been described as forming a link between the worlds of politics and administration, and successive British experiments with bureaucratic 'irregulars' are loosely modelled upon them. Interestingly, however, politicisation of the civil service in France has not led to any reduction in complaints concerning the civil service's political unresponsiveness. On the contrary, such complaints have been commonplace historically. In recent years they have been made with monotonous regularity by successive governments in the Fifth Republic, whether right, centre or left-wing.

However, owing to its historical experience – unique among

First World states – it is in the USA that politicisation of the higher civil service has gone furthest. The American president possesses powers of appointment and dismissal over about 2,000 senior civil service posts and over about 20,000 jobs in the vast federal bureaucracy in all. In the USA political appointments are made not only to a few very senior or very sensitive posts, as in other First World states, but well down into the bureaucracy. This makes it uniquely difficult to discover where the government or political executive ends and the civil service or bureaucratic executive begins. Since the inauguration of the republic, all American presidents – in the absence of any instructions to the contrary in the constitution – have rewarded their supporters with posts in the government. However it was the seventh president, Andrew Jackson (1829–37), who fully developed this 'spoils' system – the rule that the victors own the spoils of the enemy – by replacing approximately one fifth of the federal bureaucracy with his own men. Since the Civil Service Act of 1883, which sought to reform an increasingly corrupt and inefficient bureaucracy, this power of appointment has been regularised. That Act established a Civil Service Commission to recruit the bulk of the service on the basis of competitive examinations, and to operate a system of promotion by merit. It also gave security of tenure to the bulk of the service, and approximately 85 per cent of civil servants are now recruited and serve under its terms.

In theory, the US system reflects a separation of functions as well as of personnel, between policy-making – undertaken by political appointees – and the routine of non-political administration – undertaken by career bureaucrats. In practice, the persistent calls by American presidents for more political appointees to exercise better political control over the rest of the bureaucracy underlines the unreality of the functional aspect of this distinction. These presidential calls reflect the inevitable tensions – often outright opposition – engendered by the presence in one organisational structure of two such differently recruited groups of individuals. In an American department of state the senior career civil servants, the Bureau chiefs, are faced by a large number of nominally more senior political appointees – from the secretary of state down through under secretaries, deputy-under secretaries and assistant secretaries. However, the former are in a stronger position than their formal rank implies. Career civil servants with a long and detailed knowledge of their departments and vast experience in bureaucratic politics, clearly have a head start on political appointees. The latter's experience is, at most, of a few years duration, leaving them with many disadvantages within 'their' departments. Moreover, given the divided and institutionally competitive nature of the American political system, career civil servants can build their own sources of political power and influence beyond the presidentially controlled executive branch. In particular they can cultivate political support in the Congress through long-standing relationships with relevant committees and sub-committees and their members. For this purpose departments of state employ approximately seven hundred civil servants on liason work with the Congress to watch over legislation and to 'help' congressmen with information and advice. Furthermore, the departments can also seek support from pressure groups, who, as the departments' regular 'clients' will always be prepared to reinforce departmental claims in Congress; farming groups for example, support the claims of the Department of Agriculture, and defence industries support the Defence Department. Thus, career bureaucrats can and do take advantage of a constitution which divides responsibility for governmental decision-making and supervision of the executive branch between president and Congress. Thereby they can go a long way to negate effective presidential control over the executive branch, despite the very large number of political appointees.

Second World bureaucracies

The states of the Second World of communist regimes, in their search for effective political controls, have gone far beyond the levels of politicisation of the bureaucracy seen even in the USA. However, they have done so by adopting a quite different method of securing a political commitment. Utilising their highly disciplined and tentacular party organisations, these regimes have sought to merge politics and administration, politician and administrator, by permeating the civil service with Communist party members, and by ensuring party control over personnel and promotions. Since Communist party members either directly occupy, or at least control, all key posts in the civil service hierarchy it becomes meaningless to try to decide exactly where the government ends and the civil service begins. Career 'civil servants' in Second World states are able to move up a promotion ladder within the ministries which form the organisational basis of Second World administrations. Yet promotion to senior posts in the bureaucracy is perhaps as much, or even more, dependent on political reliability as on merit. Thus in such states internal controls over administrators are, in practice, of far less importance than the external political controls exercised by the respective communist parties.

For example, in the USSR civil servants are neither recruited by such conventional bureaucratic procedures as competitive examinations, nor are they guaranteed permanent tenure. The internal bureaucratic supervision exercised by the central establishments administration of the Finance Ministry – which has a responsibility for personnel matters as well as over more strictly fiscal concerns such as budgeting, financial records and auditing – is overshadowed by party controls over personnel affairs. Similarly, legal controls over administrative behaviour exercised by the Soviet Procurator General and his staff are equally dependent on party policy. The operations of this institution combine some of the functions of both Western-style administrative courts and ombudsmen with a responsibility for upholding 'socialist legality' within administrative organisations, and for ensuring that laws are interpreted and applied consistently by the bureaucracy. Procurators also have an authority to investigate violations of the law by individual civil servants. In the past, under party supervision – the overwhelming majority of procurators are party members – the primary concern of the procuracy has been to ensure administrative compliance with the letter of the law and with party policy. The investigation of complaints by citizens was of clearly secondary significance. However, the 1977 Soviet constitution contained a new constitutional right of citizen complaint against maladministration or adminstrative excesses. Under Article 58, 'Actions by officials that contravene the law or exceed their powers and infringe the rights of citizens, may be appealed against in a court in the manner prescribed by law.' Such complaints and any subsequent prosecution are handled by the procuracy. Only time will tell whether this clear change in party policy is likely to have a significant impact on an administrative system which has traditionally provided few remedies against administrative shortcomings.

Whether control is exercised directly or indirectly – through 'state' institutions – the CPSU has ultimate authority over Soviet bureaucracy and Soviet bureaucrats. The principal method used to enforce this authority is the *nomenklatura* which not only covers all the key decision-making posts in the bureaucracy but also relatively lowly positions with purely administrative functions. All top bureaucratic positions in the ministerial hierarchy fall under the *nomenklatura* of the Central Committee of the CPSU, while for more junior posts in the vast ministerial structure the *nomenklatura* is controlled in turn by the leading officials within the ministerial hierarchy itself. These officials are, almost without exception, CPSU members themselves. All Soviet bureaucrats of whatever seniority, are appointed, promoted, transferred and dismissed under this *nomenklatura* process. The party explicitly seeks to recruit and to sponsor administrators who combine political reliability and professional competence. As the former Soviet leader Leonid Brezhnev put it, they 'must organically combine dedication to the party with great competence, discipline with initiative and a creative approach to the business at hand.'[9]

The impact of the *nomenklatura* system on the performance of the Soviet administration appears to have been mixed. Its clear success as a mechanism for political control has to be balanced against its less certain impact on administrative and governmental efficiency. However, Western specialists on Soviet administration do tend to agree that, even if only informally, Western-style 'civil service' principles of recruitment and promotion on merit do increasingly appear to predominate in the Soviet administration. Similarly, senior Soviet bureaucrats – whose initial educational background like that of their American counterparts, tends to be scientific and technical – are increasingly both highly specialised and professionally competent. A typical career structure involves promotion within a single or closely related ministry or ministries. This pattern clearly suggests 'promotion on the basis of performance rather than political criteria.'[10] Thus, even at the very highest levels of the Soviet bureaucracy, the great majority of the ministers who make up the USSR's administrative 'government', the Council of Ministers, tend to have risen up through the administrative ranks in the ministry they head. Unlike Britain, ministers are never shifted from one portfolio to another. This increasing stress on expertise and technical competence is reinforced by institutions of further and higher education attached to each separate ministry – for example the Ministry of Agriculture possesses 99 colleges. In 1978, a management-training institute was established to undertake functions similar to its counterparts in most First World states, with the explicit aim of keeping Soviet civil servants abreast of the latest educational developments and technical innovations.

Third World bureaucracies

Interestingly, specialists in the subject increasingly stress how Soviet bureaucrats tend to behave in ways similar to their Western counterparts. Overall, the bureaucracies of Second World states have become increasingly comparable – even in terms of the social origins of their members – to Western bureaucracies. Paradoxically, bureaucracies in Third World regimes are moving in the opposite direction. Third World states inherited – albeit with variations according to colonial power – Western-style public administrations based on professionalism, internal controls and merit recruitment and promotion. Yet they have increasingly turned to overt partisan political controls and to systems of recruitment and promotion on the basis of declared political loyalty and commitment. These developments have occurred in an attempt to more effectively control bureaucratic institutions which invariably exert enormous political influence in Third World states. Colonial governments depended totally on their bureaucracies in the pre-independence period, with the development of 'political' institutions such as legislatures, local governments and political parties, frequently occurring only immediately before independence was granted. Consequently civil servants had far more experience of and skill in government than the politicians. From the perspective of the nationalist politicians who gained power on independence, the bureaucracy appeared to be manned by a powerful and privileged caste – frequently paid thirty to fifty times more than the average wage – with an authority which directly threatened their own. Hence the vehemence with which post-independence leaders of these states attacked their civil servants. 'It is our intention,' announced Kwame Nkrumah, Ghana's first post-independent leader, in 1961, 'to wipe out the disloyal elements of the civil service, even if by so doing we suffer some temporary dislocation of the service. For disloyal civil servants are no better than saboteurs.'[11]

In state after state the politicians sought to tame the bureaucracy by controlling recruitment, promotion, discipline and dismissal, frequently appointing individuals of their own tribal or ethnic group whom they felt would be personally as well as politically loyal. In general, very high levels of politicisation through partisan rather than merit appointments and promotions because the norm, with changes of government and regime resulting in radical changes in the personnel of the bureaucracy. This reflected the weakness rather than the strength of political parties and political leaders *vis à vis* their bureaucratic counterparts. The situation was particularly noticeable in the most recently independent of the Third World states, those of Africa. Here politicisation of the civil service had progressed much further and more rapidly than in Asian states, such as India, Malaysia and Ceylon (Sri Lanka). In the latter, political parties had deeper roots and politicians felt less overtly threatened by their bureaucracies.

Indeed, in a number of Third World states powerful civil services have efficiently prevented the emergence of well-organised and popular mass political parties. They have done so by controlling key offices in the government and by deliberately using these offices to prevent the emergence of organised and effective parties. Thus in Pakistan – whose powerful civil service developed from the famed imperial Indian Civil Service (ICS) – politicians were excluded in the crucial early years of independence from the vitally important political offices of governor-general (later president) and prime minister. Civil servants dominated these two posts until a military coup institutionalised bureaucratic rule in 1958. Civil servants also completely dominated the national and provincial governments, occupying important political offices at all levels of the political system.

Consequently, the 'political' leaders of Pakistan in its early, form-ative years as an independent state tended to share a penchant for bureaucratic rule, and even, in some cases, an explicit desire to return to a colonial-style party-less and paternalistic adminis-trative state. Collectively this group of powerful figures deliber-ately prevented the emergence of strong political parties and, in particular, fatally fragmented Pakistan's counterpart of India's powerful Congress Party, the Muslim League.

Moreover, even in Third World states with relatively well-organised and powerful political parties – as in the case of Mexico's Institutional Revolutionary Party (PRI), continuously in government since 1929 – there tends to be an important civil service element in the government. It is an almost impossible task to try to discover whether it is the party that has 'colonised' the civil service or whether the reverse has occurred. Indeed, a typical political career in Mexico tends to include a number of periods in bureaucratic as well as in elective posts. Presidents and members of their cabinets will, almost invariably, have served at different points in their careers in a number of minis-tries as well as holding posts within the ruling party. This fluidity and interchangeability is so great that it can be said that 'from almost any location in the political system, one could reasonably hope to move to almost any other location.'[12] When the Mexican presidency changes hands every six years, it has been estimated that well over 18,000 elective (party) positions and 25,000 appointive (bureaucratic) positions must be filled anew. It has also been calculated that only 35 per cent of the occupants of senior government and administrative posts retain their jobs from one presidency to the next! Superficially, this enormous appointive power in the hands of the leader of the ruling party would suggest a high degree of political control over the bureau-cracy. But, in practice, such is the nature of the Mexican political system, it could equally be argued that the reverse process has occurred. Certainly, Mexican political and administrative leaders – like many of their Third World counterparts, both civilian and military – tend to share an antipathy to public participation in decision-making and to uphold a technocratic or apolitical approach which seeks to avoid any 'interference' from outside bodies, whether exerted through pressure groups, legislative bodies or the mass media. In this sense Third World states, both civilian and military, radical and conservative, whether they like it or not, tend to be 'administrative states' *par excellence.*

It was inevitable – given the low levels of human and material resources available to most Third World states as a result of their economic underdevelopment – that the rapid expansion of bureaucracy and of governmental responsibilities that followed independence would lead to varying degrees of administrative inefficiency and chaos. Nevertheless the bureaucratic corruption that accompanied this chaos in so many states requires further explanation. Scholars continue to debate, often heatedly, the precise causes of this appropriation of public goods and money for private and personal gain. Nevertheless there is a growing recognition that the numerous, conflicting, explanations offered in the past for this behaviour may well all be, at least partially, correct. This assumption arises from an appreciation that corruption and corrupt behaviour may have a number of different causes and may take a number of different forms. Three causes and forms, in particular, stand out as being common to many, perhaps most, Third World states.

First, there is an economic explanation which identifies the corruption which invariably results from a situation of scarce goods and services whose distribution lies in the hands of the government bureaucracy. This form of corruption is particularly likely to occur in the case of imported manufactured and luxury goods such as cars, whose acquisition must be carefully controlled by states ever mindful of their balance of payments, and in the case of lucrative government contracts open to public tender. Fierce competition tends to occur amongst potential importers for the limited number of import licences and permits, or among contractors for government contracts that are available. Corruption, in the form of a 'black market bureaucracy', provides a form of rationing which sells these scarce items to the highest bidders. Second, there is a political explanation. This highlights the corruption inherent in political systems with relatively weak political parties and pressure groups, where the bureaucracy and other institutions of central government tend to make government policy in isolation from public or group opinion. Affected groups are then forced to attempt to influence policy-makers in their favour as the policy-makers, in the form of the bureaucracy, attempt to implement and administer centrally-made decisions. Similarly, the very weakness of political institutions may, in itself, encourage bureaucratic corruption since external political and judicial controls over the bureaucracy are likely to be weak. Equally, internal accountability, particularly financial controls, may well be unenforceable due to an absence of trained personnel such as government auditors. In the absence of such constraints bureaucrats are unlikely to behave any better than any other section of the public. As a Kenyan governmental commission on the civil service argued in 1971 'it is understandable that civil servants should have taken their opportunities like other citizens.'[13] Third, there is the corruption which stems from sociological causes and emerges from the cultures of states where 'bureaucratic' standards of behaviour – appointment on educational achievement, promotion on merit – are alien imports. Here normal and expected standards of conduct urge the bureaucrat and his political masters to show favour to their own ethnic groups and kinsmen, both in appointments to the bureaucracy and in the implementation of its decisions.

The outcome of these corrupt practices is usually two-fold – a civil service whose real incomes are far in excess of their nominal salaries, and an enormous loss of potential revenue to the state through the development of a thriving second or 'black' economy whose size and importance frequently rivals, and sometimes exceeds, that of the regular economy. The prevalence of corrupt practices, combined with widespread bureaucratic inefficiency in a context of a high degree of politicisation, lead to the emergence of public services whose structure and functioning is more reminiscent of pre-industrial forms of administration than of contemporary First World bureaucracies. Small wonder that rampant corruption is, almost invariably, a major reason cited by the world's militaries for their violent assumption of political power through a *coup d'état*.

8 Politics and the Military: The 'Armed Bureaucrats'

The political impact of the military

Professor S. E. Finer, a leading analyst of the political activities of the world's militaries, has underlined the point that armies 'have three massive political advantages over civilian organisations . . .'. These consist of a marked superiority in organisation over civilian institutions, an important emotional-symbolic status within their states, and a monopoly of arms. Added together they give these institutions an 'overwhelming superiority in the means of applying force.'[1] With their centralisation, hierarchy, discipline, highly developed systems of communication and *esprit de corps*, armies are clearly superior to civilian bodies in terms of organisation. Added to the generally high prestige, even, in some states, mystique, which accrues to the armed forces, and combined with a virtual monopoly of effective weaponry, the blend presents a truly formidable combination of political strengths.

Virtually all the world's independent states possess armies. The few states that have no formal army – the Central American state of Costa Rica is the best example – do possess its functional equivalent in the form of para-military police forces. Consequently, all contemporary regimes face a similar problem: how to maintain effective civilian control over the military. The complexity and magnitude of the problem thereby posed is graphically underlined by some statistics of military intervention in politics. A recent survey of military regimes found that, in December 1979, there were thirty-two such governments. Two years previously, in 1977, the same author records that there had been forty military governments, and at the end of 1974 thirty-eight. Whilst authorities often differ in their assessments of where military rule ends and civilian rule begins, there is widespread

Table 8.1   Military regimes

	1977	1979
Middle East and North Africa	7	7
South and South East Asia	7	4
Sub-Saharan Africa	17	14
Latin America	9	7
Total	40	32

Source: S. E. Finer, 'The Morphology of Military Regimes', in Roman Kolkowicz & Andrzej Korbonski, eds, *Soldiers, Peasants, and Bureaucrats* (George Allen & Unwin, 1982), pp. 281–309, p. 283, and p. 285

agreement that about 30 per cent of the world's states will, at any one time, be under some form of military rule. Even more striking, however, is the fact that these military regimes are very unevenly distributed geographically. They remain concentrated most heavily in Africa, Latin America, the Middle East, and, albeit to a somewhat lesser extent, in Asia – as Table 8.1 illustrates. Significantly, at the end of 1979 no First or Second World states were under military rule; and whilst more than a third of the World's states have recently experienced a period of direct military rule, almost half of the countries of the Third World have been so governed. Indeed, even this high figure seriously underestimates the military impact on Third World governments. It has been estimated that the military have intervened in the political process in approximately two-thirds of these states. In recent years, the military have ruled directly in one-third of these states, and indirectly, behind a facade of civilian rulers, have controlled another third.[2]

The heavy political predominance of the military in the states of the Third World contrasts markedly to their relative political quiescence in the First and Second Worlds. Of the First World states only three European countries have experienced successful military take-overs (*coups d'état*) since 1945: France in 1958, Greece in 1967, and Portugal in 1974. Significantly, in the French case the military merely succeeded in exchanging one civilian regime for another, leaving Greece and Portugal as the only two recent examples of military regimes in Western states. Equally significantly, the number of military coups *attempted* in these Western states has been very low, with France in 1961 and Spain in 1981 providing the only two additional cases. In the case of the states of the Second World of socialist regimes the statistics are equally, or even more, striking. Up to 1984 no Marxist-Leninist regime has been overthrown by a military coup. Until the assumption of martial law and direct military rule in Poland in 1981 no examples of successful military coups had occurred in this group of states at all. Even in this clear-cut case of intervention the military moved to save, and eventually restore, a collapsed Communist party. Moreover, apart from one clear-cut and admitted attempt at a military *coup d'état* in China in 1971, these states appear to have been remarkably free even from attempted coups.

Civilian control of the military: theory and practice

It would appear, therefore, that the Western and Eastern states of the First and Second Worlds have evolved relatively successful mechanisms and methods for ensuring ultimate civilian control over their armed forces. Not surprisingly, given the political divide between these two groups of regimes, the means adopted to achieve the shared goal of civilian control over the military differ quite markedly. In theory at least, the divide is absolute, and the two groups of states respectively exemplify two alternative 'models' of civilian control – originally termed 'objective' and 'subjective' methods by Professor Samuel Huntington, and, more recently, and more illuminatingly, re-christened the 'liberal' and the 'penetration' models by Professor Eric Nordlinger.[3] The essence of the liberal (formerly objective) model of control – exemplified by the Western states of the First World – lies in its emphasis on a clear division of labour and functions between civilian governmental institutions and military organisations. Specifically it rests on the absolute distinction between the very different, but complementary, *professional* responsibilities exercised by the two groups. Civilian governing institutions and their occupants are accorded professional responsibility for resolving social, economic and political conflicts, for making domestic and foreign policy, and for implementing and administering these policies. Military institutions and personnel are professionally trained for their responsibilities involving the application of force, whether this involves protecting the state from external aggressors or the regime against domestic violence. Further, in carrying out its professional duties and functions the military is viewed as clearly subordinate to the civilian political authorities. Its political role, even within its sphere of professional competence (on questions involving national security) is limited to the offering of advice, which may or may not be accepted by the political leadership.

The essence of the penetration (formerly subjective) model of control – exemplified by the Eastern bloc states of the Second World – lies in its stress on the deliberate permeation of the armed forces with the political ideas and beliefs of the ruling group. This is combined with and reinforced by penetration of the armed forces by politically reliable personnel. Emphasis is consequently placed on the continuing importance of the political indoctrination of the armed forces to ensure their absolute political loyalty to the regime in power. Promotion is made dependent on proof of this political loyalty as well as on criteria relating to more purely military matters. In short, whereas the liberal model stresses the fundamental importance of a depoliticised professional military, the penetration model underlines the importance of its opposite, politicisation and overt political commitment. As might be expected, this division exactly parallels the division between politicisation and professionalisation as methods of control over the civilian bureaucracy described in Chapter 7.

In practice, the choices facing contemporary regimes over strategies of civilian control are not between mutually exclusive 'models' of politicisation and professionalisation. As in the case of civilian bureaucracies, the real choice is between varying combinations and syntheses of the penetration and liberal approaches. Nor should this tendency to combine apparent opposites seem surprising. Thoroughly 'professional' armed forces from countries such as France, Germany and Japan have been tempted to intervene overtly in the political process during the present century. At the other end of the spectrum, a completely politicised army could easily lose its coherence and effectiveness as a fighting and, indeed, an administrative force. For instance, the Chinese military, frequently cited as a classical example of a politicised force, has, at times, devoted fully 40 per cent of their soldiers' time to political indoctrination, with some rather bizarre results. An Air Force plane maintenance conference once concluded that political thought was 'the soul of plane maintenance work . . . Marxism-Leninism could drive out mechanical malfunctions.'[4]

Thus, whilst the Liberal democracies of the First World emphasise professionalism as a method of control, and the socialist states of the Second World stress politicisation and political loyalty, these emphases are not mutually exclusive. In practice, under normal circumstances the militaries both in the liberal democracies of the First World and in the socialist states of the Second World tend to play relatively similar roles in the political process. This similarity is exemplified by the substantial agreement between President Eisenhower of the USA and the Soviet leader Nikita Khrushchev over the enormous political influence wielded by their respective militaries, and indeed, by their military-industrial complexes – to use the term that President Eisenhower made part of the political vocabulary. When the two leaders discussed the subject in 1959, Khrushchev recorded how representatives of the military would confront him with the information that the Americans were developing new weapons systems. When the Soviet leader pleaded an absence of money to match these developments they would say, 'If we don't get the money we need and if there's a war, then the enemy will have superiority over us.' 'So', concluded Khrushchev, 'we discuss it some more and we end up giving them the money they ask for.' Small wonder, therefore, that President Eisenhower's vague and cryptic warning in his farewell message about the potential dangers of the 'conjunction of an immense military establishment and a large arms industry' was echoed, albeit more explicitly, by Khrushchev in his *Memoirs*. 'Who, in our country . . .', he asked, 'can intimidate the leadership? They are the military . . .'[5]

The detailed investigations which followed President Eisenhower's often-quoted remarks revealed that he was right in his stress on the importance of the military-industrial complex in the American political process. Moreover, the available evidence reveals an equally large military-industrial complex, based on a similar alliance between the military, ministries manufacturing for military use, and other defence-related industries, in the USSR. This alliance is often termed the 'steel eaters' or the 'metal eaters', due to its heavy industrial bias. It campaigns for a concentration of available resources into defence spending and defence-related industrialisation. Conversely it opposes any major budgetary movements away from these priorities, and towards in particular, increased consumer satisfaction, or 'goulash Communism'. This military-industrial complex in turn underpins the world's largest peacetime army. The budgetary priority given to these forces graphically underlines both their high prestige and the considerable political influence which they are accorded.

The defence industries are the most modern and developed sector of the economy, and this sector accounts for and monopolises a very high proportion of the educational, scientific, technical, managerial and labour skills in the USSR. Quite what this proportion is can only be roughly estimated since the USSR publishes only a single statistic for defence spending in its national budget. Moreover, such is the secrecy which surrounds Soviet defence expenditure that no official information is given on what activities are covered by this allocation. The inescapable conclusion is that the Soviet authorities are, quite deliberately, seeking to conceal both the scale of and trends in Soviet military expenditure. Hence it is not surprising that estimates of Soviet military expenditure have varied from 4 to 40 per cent of Gross National Product. Since the Soviet Union does not use the concept of GNP, this figure has to be estimated too! However, what is agreed is that the Soviet budget clearly understates Soviet defence expenditures and that real expenditure in any one year is between two and five times as great as stated. The American Central Intelligence Agency (CIA), estimates that the USSR devotes 11 to 12 per cent of GNP directly to military expenditure. If other expenditures related to 'national security' are included, such as the Soviet space programme, the percentage rises to 12 or 13 per cent, and other, higher, estimates have been made.

This expenditure contrasts interestingly and very markedly

with the comparable figures for the UK and the USA, which, in 1981, were 5.7 per cent (for the UK) and 6.2 per cent (USA). Nevertheless, since the GNP of the USA is over twice as great as that of the USSR, the overall gap between American and Soviet military expenditures, although marked, is much less than percentage figures suggest. The US Arms Control and Disarmament Agency (ACDA), has estimated that in 1978 the USSR spent 153.6 billion US dollars and the USA 108.4 billion U.S. dollars. Over the ten-year period 1968–1978 it has been estimated that Soviet military spending exceeded American spending by over 10 per cent. However, since the USSR not only has a much smaller GNP than the USA but also a larger population (263.5 million in 1979 compared to 225 million), the overall impact of military expenditure on the balance and performance of the economy is clearly much greater. In particular the military consumes the output from certain key industries to a very marked extent. In the case of the crucial machine-building and metal-working industry – which supplies investment goods in the form of machines and equipment to the rest of the Soviet economy – the CIA estimates the defence share at 30 per cent, and other estimates have been even higher.[6] In this context it is illuminating to find that Khrushchev and Brezhnev, two Soviet leaders of very different political temperaments, shared similar views on the impact of high military expenditures on the economy. The former stressed in his *Memoirs* how 'today, as yesterday, the most unproductive expenditures of all are those made on the armed forces.' The latter underlined to a military audience in 1963, 'how dearly we must pay in resources and energies to support and arm a modern army.'[7]

Military intervention: varieties and forms

What must be underlined is that civilian control of the military is always a question of degree. *All* militaries are involved in politics, but the *extent* which this is so varies. Thus, individual militaries can be placed on a continuum or scale of involvement in the political process. The significant points on this continuum – where the power and impact of the military relative to the power and impact of civilian institutions on policy-making clearly changes – can be easily identified. These different 'levels' of

Figure 8.1   Levels of military involvement in the political process

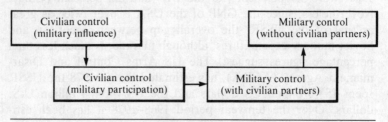

Source: Adapted from C. E. Welch, Jr,, Ed, *Civilian Control of the Military* (State University of New York Press, 1976), p. 3.

military intervention in the political process can conveniently be expressed in a simple diagram (see Figure 8.1).

Military 'influence' within a context of overall civilian control, is exemplified by the experiences of the regimes of the contemporary First World. In these regimes the military is not excluded from politics, but its political influence occurs through accepted institutional channels. Overall the military plays the role of a powerful bureaucratic pressure group. This political impact is dependent not on the use of the military's coercive fire-power, but upon its specialist expertise and its technical abilities. These ensure that the military is able to influence political decisions as the possessor of important skills and vital information.

Military 'participation' in politics approximates to the situation which exists in the Second World of the communist states where a situation of overall civilian control exists, but the military plays a more variable and changeable role in the political process. In these regimes, the military exercises 'influence' under normal conditions, but participates more overtly and directly in decision-making under conditions of crisis, such as major intra-party disputes or leadership successions. Pressure group activity may then be replaced by veiled coercive threats or political blackmail. Under such conditions of crisis, and frequently at the prompting of individual civilians or political factions, the military may come to exercise a veto power over policy-making. Additionally, it may increasingly occupy key roles in the political process – as in contemporary Poland.

With the third stage, – the military 'control' of politics, which is rarely reached outside the Third World – any veneer of effective civilian control disappears. The military typically deposes and dispenses with the civilian leadership entirely, and commonly replaces it with a military regime. Such regimes may be of two broad types. In the first and commonest form, the armed forces do not rule alone but with civilian partners, and the resultant military-civilian coalition may in fact be weighted numerically in favour of the latter. Nevertheless, however veiled the power of the military, its real governing role is clear. Alternatively, the military may form a ruling *junta* exclusively from its own ranks, relegating civilians to an overtly subordinate role. In practice, exclusively military juntas are relatively uncommon, and even those with a predominantly military executive (90 per cent or more) exist in only about 15 per cent of military regimes. In about 80 per cent of such regimes, either a mixed civilian-military executive exists (approximately 40 per cent), or an exclusively military council is counterbalanced by a mixed civilian-military cabinet (approximately 40 per cent).[8] In all cases, however, a military officer initially assumes the position of chief executive, whether he is chairman of the council, prime minister or president. In all cases the hallmark of a military regime is effective (if not always numerical) military predominance over civilians in the executive.

The above picture suggests a very sharp divide between military and civilian regimes. Specifically it presupposes that military rule typically occurs as the result of the sudden and violent deposition of a civilian regime by a deliberate *coup d'état*. However, as might be anticipated in the complicated world of modern politics, there is in some cases an imperceptible divide between the two types of system. For example, a number of contemporary regimes in the Third World possess civilian chief executives or heads of state who have been legally and constitutionally appointed, but who rely heavily for their political survival on the support of their militaries – as in the case of a number of Near and Middle Eastern monarchies, notably those of Jordan and Morocco. Another recent example is provided by the Philippines Republic, where President Marcos ruled by martial law and decree from 1972 to 1986 without any effective control from political or judicial institutions, engineering a new constitution which made him president, prime minister, commander-in-chief of the armed forces, and martial law administrator. Similarly in Central American states, such as El Salvador, Guatamala and Panama, civilian rule has merely been a facade and the real arbiters of power remain the respective militaries.

Nevertheless, despite these ambiguous cases of regimes on or near the borderline of the military/civilian divide, 'military regimes proper', to borrow Finer's term, are those whose installation followed an unconstitutional, and occasionally bloody, military coup.[9] This is the process by which all of the thirty-two governments, which were identified earlier in this chapter as military regimes in 1979, came to power. Among Third World states, and, particularly those in Latin America and Africa, military coups are so common as to seem a perfectly normal and routine way of changing governments and rulers – more common, indeed, than elections. After a century and a half of military interventions, Latin Americans are so familiar with the phenomenon of the *coup d'état* that they have developed a sophisticated vocabulary to describe precisely the different forms that such interventions take, as well as the different stages in the proceedings. Accordingly, coups in Third World states follow a well tried pattern, and this collective wisdom has even been distilled into 'a practical handbook' for coup-makers![10] Indeed, with all this collective experience it may seem surprising that between 30 per cent and 50 per cent of attempted coups fail. Nevertheless, these high numbers of failures underline the important point that only well planned and well executed conspiracies will succeed, and that what might appear to be a relatively simple exercise in most Third World states requires much careful preparation.

Explaining military coups

Why, it must be asked, does civilian control over the military fail so frequently and so dramatically in the contemporary Third World? What are the causes of this proliferation of military coups? To these questions a short and simple answer can be given. Military coups occur because civilian rule has ceased to appear legitimate to the armed forces. However, this simple formulation clearly requires further elaboration to convincingly account for such a widespread method of changing governments and regimes. In particular, two further questions immediately present themselves. How do civilian regimes and governments lose their legitimacy? What reasons will convince the military that civilian governments should not only cease to be supported, but should be forcibly removed?

These crucial questions, as to when and under what circumstances the military is likely to become convinced of a government's illegitimacy, are perhaps most easily answered by first looking at the way the existence of a legitimate government will inhibit military intervention. In states where the majority of the population believes that the government has a moral right to govern, and where there is a strong attachment to civilian institutions, there exists a moral barrier to military intervention. In such states interventions would be condemned as usurpations. Moreover, this barrier is not merely a moral one. Military intervention in such states would be likely to trigger sufficient resistance, both violent and non-violent, to create serious problems in the maintenance of order, and to lead to bitter disputes *within* the military about the rectitude of the military's actions. Conversely, where the majority of the population believes that the government does not have a moral right to govern, where few believe that its laws and commands should be obeyed, where its authority is questioned, and where its allegiance is rejected, no such barriers exist to military intervention. In such cases intervention would be regarded not as usurpation but as salvation, and would be met with gratitude rather than resentment or resistance.

Under what circumstances, then, do civilian governments lose their legitimacy, their moral right to rule? Although circumstances vary widely, governmental legitimacy and support for civilian institutions are most commonly undermined by the failure of these individuals and institutions to perform their tasks satisfactorily. In particular the inability to cope with problems in three broad areas are likely to be crucial: the maintenance of stability and order, economic management, and upholding legal and constitutional standards of behaviour. Significantly, the three most common accusations made by militaries after they have undertaken a coup concern the unconstitutional and illegal behaviour, and particularly the widespread political corruption, of the civilian rulers; their responsibility for economic stagnation or failures such as rising unemployment or rampant inflation; and their inability to cope with protest or opposition before it escalates into violence and disorder. However, it would clearly be naive to assume that military self-justifications are likely to reveal *all* the reasons for their interventions. In particular, a concentration on the manner in which militaries are *pulled* into interventions by the failures of the civilian rulers should not blind us to the likelihood that, in most, if not all, cases armed forces are likely to *push* for intervention for reasons of their own. Indeed, in analyses of military coups in the Third World, purely selfish motivations and the desire to protect the corporate identity and privileges of the army have rightly been emphasised.

In general terms, it may be suggested that these corporate and selfish motivations for coups are an important influences on their timing. Although such reasons usually provide only a partial explanation as to *why* the military intervenes, they are frequently crucial in determining exactly *when* a coup occurs. In particular, they help explain how the military as an institution, or corporate entity, comes to openly reject the legitimacy of civilian institutions and rulers. Armed forces, like all other public institutions, seek to protect their own vital interests, which can in turn be defined and specified in terms of adequate budgets; control over their internal management; the prevention of rival institutions from either encroaching on their responsibilities or usurping their functions; and the avoidance of any threats to the continued existence of the military as a separate and autonomous organisation. Threats, especially of a serious or persistent nature, to one or more of these corporate interests are likely to be met by a coup. Thus the regularity with which military regimes increase military budgets after coups in Third World states, by, on average, between 50 per cent and 75 per cent, suggests that budgetary threats are important to militaries. However, they are clearly less important than the other three corporate motives in triggering coups. In particular, there are widespread and numerous Third World examples of coups sparked off by governmental attempts to increase their political control over the military through interfering with aspects of internal management. Governments have often interfered with training, promotions and postings. Many have challenged the military's monopoly of control over external and internal security by recruiting a separate élite corps or paramilitary force. Some have even challenged the military's very existence by threatening its disbandment and replacement by a citizens' militia or 'people's army'. Since the legitimacy of most Third World regimes is precarious – with many beset by acute combinations of economic problems and social unrest, and with governments frequently rife with corruption – military perceptions of the need for a fresh start, however selfishly based and motivated, are seldom greatly out of tune with the attitudes of a substantial proportion of the population.

Military rule and its consequences
However, if the inauguration of military rule is a time of relative optimism for many Third World states, disillusion is soon likely to set in. The evidence suggests that the resultant military regimes seldom perform better, and generally perform worse, than their civilian predecessors and counterparts. While military regimes clearly do vary, variations are not nearly so marked as among their civilian counterparts. Military regimes are, invariably, authoritarian. They remain characteristically closed to political competition and popular participation, and seek to strictly control and limit the numbers of individuals and institutions involved in making policies. They concentrate power almost exclusively in the hands of the executive. Initially, at least, political parties are banned, the legislature suspended, the media muzzled, the judiciary curbed, and rule is by executive decree. Significantly, only approximately 15 per cent of military regimes allow legislatures any real power, and only about 15 per cent allow more than a single 'official' party to operate. In most military regimes elections, if held, are non-competitive, with the population 'encouraged' to vote *en masse* for the officially approved candidate.

The introduction of authoritarian forms of rule is clearly consistent with the characteristic political attitudes of the military, which tend to be conservative. As the historian Alfred

Vagts argues, an army is generally 'conservative in relation to the order in which it thrives, whether that order be agrarian, capitalistic, or communistic.'[11] In general, military men have a characteristically apolitical or antipolitical attitude toward problems of government. In particular, they tend to view political competition as divisive and selfish, and to regard all forms of political activity as potential threats to public order and good government. This 'politics of wanting to be above politics' manifests itself most clearly in an antipathy to party politics. Indeed, it has been suggested that 'if the military of the new nations has an ideology, it is distaste for party politics.'[12] This distaste leads directly to a choice of governing methods and institutions which centre on administrative solutions and executive structures, and which denigrate the ideas of bargaining, compromise, and participation. 'The military man, by his intellectual formation', argues a retired Peruvian major, 'is not oriented to discussion. His long custom of commanding and obeying incapacitates him to construct a democratic government.'[13]

Moreover, this administrative and managerial view of government is reinforced by the limited aims of most military regimes. It has been estimated that only approximately 10 per cent of military rulers seek either to control governments over the long term, or to achieve long-term political and economic goals. Characteristically, most military regimes promise to return power to civilians within a few years, *after* they have purged the corrupt and restored the state politically and economically. Broadly speaking, this is one promise that military regimes do tend to keep since such regimes have an average life span of only about five years. However the real incentive to return to the barracks is perhaps less likely to be due to the success of the military in solving persistent problems, than to the divisions and disputes within the armed forces which a period of governmental power reveals and exacerbates. The record suggests that only rarely are military regimes able to achieve long-term legitimacy, and are accorded a moral right to govern by those they rule. Nor should this seem surprising, since military claims to bring high standards of honesty to government are seldom realised. Military regimes are, by and large, as corrupt as civilian ones. In the West African state of Ghana, for example, only two years of military rule were needed to convince the populace of the underlying similarity between military and civilian rulers in their standards of honesty. 'The Cars are the Same, Only the Drivers have Changed' was the title of a very popular, but swiftly banned, record. Moreover, the widespread military hostility to popular political participation, their élitist attitude to government, and their particular antipathy to party politics, inevitably affects their ability to develop political institutions. Without such institutions militaries are generally unable to build on their initial popularity as cleaners of the Augean stables of government, and fail to develop long-term mass support and legitimacy.

Military regimes are pre-eminently bureaucratic systems of government. Armed forces were referred to in the chapter title as 'armed bureaucrats' and this depiction aptly describes both the style of decision-making in military regimes and the characteristic structures of rule in essentially administrative states. The two bureaucratic groups tend to share similar perspectives on politics and decision-making and 'military' government characteristically takes the form of a coalition between military and civil service. For example, in Nigeria, Africa's most populous state, almost all important decisions under military rule between 1966 and 1979 were made by a group of half a dozen senior military officers with a few civil servants acting as advisers. Similar coalitions exist in other military regimes. For example, military rule in Brazil, one of the most economically advanced of Third World states, has characteristically taken the form of an alliance between the military and technocrats – technically trained administrators, such as economists, lawyers and engineers. Only rarely is the power of civil servants reduced under military regimes. Whilst it is the 'armed bureaucrats' who remain pre-eminent, civil servants tend to occupy prominent positions not only as advisers but also as decision-makers.

The cyclical pattern of coup, military rule, disengagement, civilian rule, and coup can be most clearly seen in Latin America, where military intervention has been endemic for up to a century and a half since independence. However it is a pattern that is also becoming increasingly obvious in the more recently independent states of the Third World, particularly those in Africa. The first successful coup breaks moral barriers to military intervention and opens the flood-gates. Significantly, the agonies among military men that preceded the first coup are seldom repeated for subsequent takeovers. The first coup usually occurs primarily for understandable reasons associated with the poor performance of the civilian regime. Subsequent coups often occur for far more cynical reasons, associated increasingly not only with the corporate desires of the military but also with the personal ambitions or fears of individual soldiers. Only the dismal failures of successive military governments and a rising tide of opposition to military rule can break this vicious circle. Even then the subsequent performance of the civilians may be such as to quickly engender another coup and the start of another cycle of interventions. Thus, in the cases of two former British West African colonies, Ghana and Nigeria, independence was followed by less than a decade of civilian rule. Subsequently, Nigeria, during continuous military rule from 1966–1979, passed through a long and bloody civil war, as well as four different military leaders and governments. Significantly, despite the widespread popularity of the return to civilian rule in 1979, Nigeria returned to military rule again on New Year's Eve 1983. Once again, civilian rule had rapidly lost its legitimacy and credibility, both in the eyes of the people and the armed forces. Ghana, following a brief period of military rule (1966–1969), returned power to civilians only to see a discredited civilian regime removed again in 1972. After this date military rule, amid further coups and coup attempts, lasted, under three different military governments, until its bloody demise in 1979. Under pressure from lower ranks in the armed forces, three former military heads of state were among eight senior military officers executed for corruption. Power was then surrendered, temporarily, by the military to civilian leaders. This civilian interlude, however, lasted only until New Year's Eve 1981 when the military returned to power once more in a bankrupt state which had become notorious for its corruption and inefficiency.

The existence of such cycles of intervention and disengagement should further alert us to appreciate that an absence (whether temporary or permanent) of overt signs does not mean that the military plays no role in the political process. Some of the world's militaries, notably those in the stable regimes of the First and

Second Worlds, have consistently accepted and supported civilian governments and have upheld the legitimacy of civilian control over the armed forces. Some, notably in the Third World, have not done so. Nonetheless, *all* the world's militaries play an important (if variable) role in the political process. Indeed the frequently used metaphors of the iceberg and the river are particularly apt in illustrating the nature of the political impact of the world's armed forces. Despite the fact that the visible tip of the iceberg or the surface of the river – military coups and army rule – impresses itself on our attention, most of the political activities of the world's militaries occur, like the bulk of the iceberg and the flow of the river, beneath the surface and out of sight.

9 Conclusion: Regimes Revisited

governments and have again the legitimacy of civilian control over the armed forces, some regimes in the Third World have not done so. Nonetheless, while the world's militaries play an important (if variable) role in the political process. Indeed the frequently used metaphors of the 'midwife' and the 'fireman' are particularly apt in illustrating the nature of the political impact of the world's armed forces. Despite the fact that the visible tip

In the introductory chapter, where contemporary regimes were divided, albeit tentatively, into three categories – First World, Second World, Third World – the promise was made to return once again in the final chapter to a further consideration of their different characteristics. This re-examination of the different styles of government practised in the three types of regimes highlights some of the problems of evaluation and of judgment involved in any classification of the world's governments. A consideration of these problems not only raises further important questions about the nature of comparative political analysis, but also provides a useful indication of the perennial, and often fierce, academic disputes which pervade the field.

First World regimes
Ideologically the states of the First World pattern are characterised by a commitment to liberal-democracy. This commitment refers much less to a series of aspirations to be realised in the future, than to a claim to encourage, in the present, open political processes which allow free play to all individuals and social forces or organisations. In particular, as democracies, the regimes of the First World would claim to exhibit their desire to be responsive to the demands of their citizens by providing for competitive elections, with all adults eligible to vote, and for basic civil and political freedoms. Such competitive elections can offer a genuine choice to voters, not just of candidates but of different political parties with alternative policies and programmes. Moreover, the record of First World states in actually achieving some alteration of the party composition of their governments is generally good. In only a handful of the approximately thirty states which were described as comprising the First World pattern

has the same party continually achieved and sustained a governing majority over more than a ten-year period. If elections did not lead directly to the kind of clear-cut governmental changes exhibited in British or American-style two-party systems, inter-party bargaining in multi-party systems has often had a comparable effect in ensuring some turnover in the party in power. As a result in most of the 'contemporary democracies' analysed in detail by G. Bingham Powell 'most substantial parties did get to share power' at some point during the two decades between 1960 and 1980.[1] Only in Japan, France and Italy were parties which regularly won over 20 per cent of the vote excluded from power throughout this period. Interestingly, the party so excluded in France, the Communist Party (PCF), joined a governmental coalition with the Socialists in 1981. Similarly, the excluded Italian Communist Party (PCI) formed a governing legislative coalition with the ruling Christian Democrats *without* being granted cabinet posts between 1977 and 1979. Moreover, the available evidence, though rather limited and tentative, also suggests that this characteristic First World responsiveness to shifts in public opinion extends beyond the composition of governments to the policies that these governments subsequently pursue. For example, in the contemporary democracies examined by Powell, the changes of party control of government brought about by periodic elections revealed significant effects on the policies pursued in such varied fields as abortion law, redistribution of income and the growth of the government itself.

Basic civil and political freedoms, and especially the ability to freely engage in political activity, secured by a free press and other mass media and by an impartial police force and judiciary, are equally essential features and under-pinnnings of genuine democracy. Without such basic freedoms, effective and genuine representative democracy is unworkable and free electoral competition disappears. Significantly, the states of the First World tend to score consistently highly on indexes of political and civil rights. The Freedom House organisation ranks all the world's states annually on these dimensions. Their political rights index measures the extent to which citizens are allowed to play an active and critical part in the selection of their political leaders, and the extent to which political parties may be freely formed. On this dimension, almost all First World states have consistently been ranked at, or very close to, the top since the institution of these surveys in 1973. Similarly high scores are also achieved by most First World states on the civil rights index. This seeks to measure the extent to which people are able to openly express their views without fear of reprisals from the state, and are protected by a free press and an independent judiciary.

Thus, among First World regimes the accepted concept of freedom tends to assume that state and society are clearly distinguished. Consequently, it tends also to be accepted in these regimes that social institutions, such as the press and other mass media, the universities and the trade unions, will be accorded a sufficient degree of political independence and freedom from state control to allow them to operate autonomously in the political process. Overall, it is accepted among First World states that individual participation in the political process – especially voting to decide on the composition of legislatures and political executives – will be buttressed by the freely chosen political participation of a large number of basically autonomous non-governmental organisations. These organisations, principally in the form of the parties and pressure groups discussed in Chapters 5 and 6, participate in policy-making in a process often termed pluralist. A 'pluralist state' can be defined as one in which many, relatively autonomous, politically significant groups exist and operate, and in which any one individual is likely to belong to, or identify with, a number of these groups. Thus pluralism, as Robert Dahl points out, tends to 'refer to *organisational* pluralism, that is to the existence of a plurality of relatively autonomous (independent) organisations . . . within the domain of a state.' Clearly, the existence of pluralism depends not so much on the existence of many competing organisations and groups – all regimes possess these in some form or another – but on what Dahl has termed their 'relative autonomy'.[2]

Empirically, the pluralist democracies analysed by Professor Dahl form a category corresponding almost exactly to G. Bingham Powell's list of contemporary democracies presented in Chapter 1. Both, in turn, coincide with the First World regime pattern under consideration here. In the approximately thirty contemporary pluralist democracies relative autonomy, or freedom from state control, is possessed by what Professor Dahl terms governmental, political and economic organisations. In the first place, the major institutions of central government – political and bureaucratic executives, legislatures and judiciaries – are in important ways, if to markedly different degrees in different states, independent of each other. Local governments, similarly, tend to enjoy some independence – again with variations of degree. In the second place, a large variety of political associations, particularly in the form of parties and pressure groups, interact in varied and complex fashions with governmental organisations in the making and the implementation of public policy in different states. They also maintain a crucial degree of autonomy. Third, economic organisations, in the form of business firms and trade unions, maintain a relative autonomy from the state. The former often make important decisions that are not controlled by governments. Similarly, 'independent trade unions that exercise the right to strike exist in all democratic countries' and by so doing underline their relative autonomy.[3]

Second World regimes

Conversely, it is the absence of any meaningful 'relative autonomy', at least for non-governmental organisations, which clearly differentiates the states of the socialist Second World from the genuinely 'pluralist' states of the First World. This is not to suggest that certain features or elements of pluralism cannot easily be identified within states like the Soviet Union – particularly in terms of the clash of organisations, and of the prevalent group conflicts within the governmental and party institutions which comprise the Soviet state and regime, described earlier in this book. However, these admitted elements of pluralism or 'pluralist aspects' do not make the USSR a 'pluralist state', since the political and economic organisations described by Professor Dahl – political parties and pressure groups – either remain firmly under state control or themselves form a permanent part of the state and of the governmental structure. Consequently, their achievement of Dahl's 'relative autonomy' is impossible under present conditions. Significantly, wherever and whenever, as for example in Czechoslovakia in 1968 and in Poland in 1980–81, states in Soviet dominated Eastern Europe appeared to approximate to full 'organisational pluralism' the USSR has ensured, directly or indirectly, the abrupt termination of such experiments. Equally significantly, among the regimes of the Second World, it is Yugoslavia which currently approximates most closely to a state of organisational pluralism, and Yugoslavia lies outside the USSR's immediate sphere of political, military and economic influence.

Consequently, the question (raised but deliberately left aside in Chapter 6) as to whether the Soviet Union can correctly be described as 'pluralist' can now be answered negatively. Moreover, this answer coincides with that given by Soviet theorists, in whose writings and speeches there is 'nothing but contemptuous dismissal for the whole idea', which they appear to find 'abusive'. Thus pluralism and its allowance of the free and open play of political forces has been described as 'deeply alien to Soviet people' who live in a society characterised not by diversity but by 'political unity and popular power'. 'Communism,' stressed L. F. Ilyichev the Communist party's chief of propaganda under Khrushchev 'is a highly organised society, a society of organised and therefore of strict discipline.' This theme was taken up by former party leader. Leonid Brezhnev 'Comrades, what we are building is the most organised and most hard-working society in the history of mankind.' The whole idea of pluralism, suggest Hill and Frank, appears 'too close to anarchy to a party whose programme declaims the need for planning if society is to develop.'[4]

According to the ideology of Marxism-Leninism, as authoritatively interpreted and reinterpreted by the ruling Communist party, the USSR, like other Second World states, is seen as progressively moving towards a specific goal – the achievement of communism. This idea of politics as a constant movement in a specific, preordained, direction contrasts markedly to the First World liberal-democratic view of the aims and objectives of political activity. In the latter group of states the essence of political activity is viewed as the peaceful solution of the inevitable conflicts which arise in any social grouping. In Second World liberal-democratic view of the aims and objectives of and mobilising the population to achieve the goals specified by the ruling 'vanguard' party and sanctified by the official ideology.

Thus the Soviet writers V. M. Lesnyi and N. V. Chernogolovkin explicitly describe the role of the CPSU in terms of 'the mobilisation and organisation of people for fulfilling state plans and directives of the party and government.' 'Spontaneity,' declared Khrushchev, 'is the deadliest enemy of all...' and its avoidance, at all costs, explains the USSR's obsessive concern with organisational and personal conformity.[5] In the first place, the whole competitive process centred on open multi-party and pressure group activity is missing from Second World states. Additionally, representative institutions, official and voluntary economic, social and cultural organisations, and the media of communications are all expected – and encouraged through the operation of democratic centralism – to present a united front in support of governmental policy rather than to press for their own separate interests. Consequently, the occupants of the central institutions of party and government in Second World states are able to formulate policy without any need to involve – unless they so wish – non-governmental organisations in the process. They are also able to involve the same organisations directly in the process of policy application and implementation, as 'transmission belts' for the dissemination and enforcement of those policies deemed to be in the general interest by the party leadership.

From this perspective, therefore, the relative political uniformity and conformity of Second World states contrasts markedly to the relative political diversity – expressed both in the form of competing political parties and a multitude of pressure groups – exhibited by their First World counterparts. Equally, the two groups of states also contrast markedly in the extent to which political power is centralised and concentrated both institutionally and personally. In First World states – despite varying degrees of executive ascendancy – the influence of the political and bureaucratic executive (or the central government and administration) is counterbalanced, albeit to varying degrees; legislative and judicial institutions and regional or local governments as well as numerous non-governmental organisations, all possess significant degrees of political influence. In Second World states, the institutions and organisations of *major* significance for political decision-making are, in practice if not in theory, much fewer. Political power is heavily concentrated in the hands of the small number of individuals who are primarily the occupants of senior party posts. The same individuals also tend to play key controlling roles in 'state' legislative and executive institutions – for example by concurrently occupying posts in the Presidia of either the Supreme Soviet or the Council of Ministers in the USSR. It is *possible* to argue that First World states are, in practice, similarly dominated by a 'power élite' – in the sense that relatively small numbers of individuals in relation to the total population dominate key public and private sector decision-making institutions. However, the existence of competitive national elections ensures that potential members of the political élite, at least, are directly accountable to the mass of the people for their actions. This 'democratic élitism' contrasts markedly to the absence of public accountability in Second World states. Here, party leaders are in theory elected by the party membership, but are in practice self-selected through the *Nomenklatura* process and the operation of the discipline of democratic centralism.

The promise in Party Rule 19, defining 'democratic centralism' in the CPSU, that 'all leading party bodies are elected', whilst correct in form is somewhat misleading in substance. For it is only at the lowest level of the party's institutional hierarchy, the PPOs, that the ordinary party member has a right to vote directly on the subject of his representation at town or district party conferences, on the composition of the bureau or committee which effectively controls party activities at every level, and on the crucial question as to who will become the local party secretary. Interestingly, very few PPO secretaries are defeated in these ballots. For example, it was reported that in 1979 of approximately 400,000 individuals standing for these posts only 88 were defeated. Above this lowest level of the PPO, all party elections are indirect, and as the election and the institution involved becomes more important the proportions of the party membership involved grow progressively smaller. Thus, delegates to the party conferences which are periodically held in all the territorial units into which the party is divided – rising in political importance from the districts through provinces, cities and territories to the five-yearly party conferences held in each union republic – are all formally selected by the delegates to the conferences or congresses at the level immediately below them. Thus it is union republic delegates who, in turn, select the delegates to the All-Union Party Congress.

The delegates to these conferences and congresses are also entrusted with the extremely important task of formally electing the party's 'leading organs', or controlling individuals and institutions, at every territorial level – including the highest national or 'All-Union' level, when the Congress formally elects a Central Committee which, in turn, elects the Politburo and Secretariat. Thus, ordinary party members play no direct part in the 'election' of the party's leaders and in decisions on the membership of the party's central institutions. Indeed it is somewhat misleading to describe the process involved in choosing the occupants of major party posts in the USSR as elections at all. Self-selection and self-perpetuation are a much more accurate description of what actually occurs. Although these processes are conducted in secrecy it is clear – and consistent with the norms of democratic centralism and the requirements of the *nomenklatura* – that all CPSU 'elections' are carefully controlled by the party leadership who clearly choose the composition of party institutions in advance. 'On paper,' concludes Jerry Hough, 'the selection procedures inside the party seem democratic: in practice the votes at each stage of this process are taken unanimously.'[6] Consequently, enormous power rests in the hands of those few individuals in the party Secretariat who control this personnel selection process, and particularly in the hands of the party leader, who presides over the Secretariat's operations.

In fact this centrally controlled system of selection has been described as the main basis of the power that the party leader possesses. This power is most clearly evidenced by the great difficulty of removing and replacing successive party leaders, however old and infirm. All, with the sole exception of Nikita Khrushchev, have died in office. The party's general secretary presides over a process which has been termed 'a circular flow of power' through which, by controlling appointments and elections, he is able to control the party Congress and therefore the composition of the Central Committee and its Politburo.[7] This situation leads to a reversal of expectations about the power of political leaders based on Western, First World, experience.

First World leaders, whose mandate is based on national elections, are at their most powerful and most influential when this mandate is relatively fresh – shortly after their election or re-election. This situation is characterised by the existence of a 'honeymoon' period early in a term of office when the leader can most easily claim popular support for the policies on which he has campaigned and been elected, or a more general 'mandate' to govern. Whilst the impact of this period is most clearly exhibited in the American presidential system, it is also characteristic of British-style parliamentary systems, despite their disciplined party majorities. Second World leaders, on the other hand, are able to increase their power gradually during their periods in office as they are able to progressively fill important posts with their own supporters. Conversely, Second World leaders are at their weakest when First World leaders have most authority and influence, shortly after their assumption of office. For their initial selection is in the hands of a relatively small group of politicians – appropriately termed the Soviet 'selectorate' by Archie Brown[8] – who almost certainly owed their posts, if not always their entire loyalty, to the previous party leader. Thus, Soviet party leaders are chosen by the Politburo in consultation with members of the Secretariat, with this choice subject to ratification by the full Central Committee.

It is these same institutions which are involved if, as in the case of Khrushchev in 1964, a general secretary is to be removed during his period in office. Consequently the party leader will obviously make personnel selection to these key institutions a high priority, and will seek, if and when he can, to 'pack' these key organs with known supporters. Initially, however, the general secretary 'inherits' a group of senior party figures he has not chosen, and who cannot quickly be changed, but with whom he must co-operate closely in Politburo and Secretariat. This contrasts markedly with the almost complete personal power of an American president over his choice of cabinet. How soon the Soviet party leader can place his own men in the highest posts is more dependent on luck than political acumen. For example, in fifteen months in office between November 1982 and February 1984 Yuri Andropov was able to take advantage, before his own demise, of the almost simultaneous deaths of a number of ageing party figures. Consequently he was able to replace one-sixth of the top leadership group in the Politburo and Secretariat – a more substantial turnover than any of his predecessors had ever achieved in so short a time.

Once in power, however, Soviet party leaders are much more likely to die in office than be evicted from it. Their long-term power over personnel selection ensures that their removal is almost impossible, short of a general revolt by their fellow-leaders, and their resignation, apparently, unthinkable. The power that control over the selection of key personnel eventually gives Soviet party leaders is well illustrated by the fact that since 1917 there have been only seven undisputed Soviet leaders. Of Mikhail Gorbachov's six predecessors five – Lenin, Stalin, Brezhnev, Andropov, and, most recently, Chernenko – died in office, while only one – Khrushchev – was removed from office. In this respect, there is a marked contrast with First World states where leadership turnover tends to be high, as parties and party leaders win and then lose popular and electoral support. In the USA, for example, where an official maximum of two four-year terms now sets a constitutional limit to presidential tenure of office, there have been nine different presidents since 1932. Of the eight presidents who preceded Ronald Reagan, two – Truman and Johnson – did not seek re-election for a second term, fearing electoral defeat. Two – Ford and Carter – were defeated seeking re-election. One – Nixon – was forced to resign. Two – Roosevelt and Kennedy – died in office. Only one – Eisenhower – actually completed his full terms of office.

Significantly, in Second World states direct elections are used only for choosing the membership of the politically less significant bodies – the national and social legislatures. Furthermore, all Second World legislative elections are in effect 'elections without choice', and their political role and importance differs markedly from the competitive elections in First World states.[9] In some of the Second World states this absence of electoral choice is complete and voters are offered only the possibility of abstention or voting for a single 'official candidate'. In others, whilst voters are offered no choice of governing party, they may either be offered some choice among individual party candidates, or even among candidates of different parties within an electoral coalition or 'Front' dominated by the ruling Communist party. For example, of the nine Eastern European communist states, five – East Germany, Hungary, Poland, Rumania and Yugoslavia – currently offer one or other of these two forms of what Alex Pravda terms 'limited-choice' elections. The other four East European states – Albania, Bulgaria, Czechoslovakia and the USSR – offer voters only a single official candidate at all elections – (although in Bulgaria and Czechoslovakia the Communist party, theoretically at least, operates as part of a coalition or 'Front'). Elections in these four states are termed 'plebiscitary' by Pravda, since they are the direct descendants of Stalinist plebiscitary elections inaugurated in 1936 in the USSR and in the early 1950s in the Soviet-dominated states of Eastern Europe. The hallmark of these elections was an unsubtle contradiction between electoral theory and electoral practice. 'On paper Stalinist plebiscitary elections were the very model of electoral rectitude.' In practice all stages of the electoral process were stage-managed to achieve the desired results.[10]

In the post-Stalin era, overt electoral coercion has disappeared, but the respective communist parties continue to exercise a controlling function. This involvement extends from the nomination of candidates acceptable to the party, through the election campaign which concentrates on national achievements, to the election itself, in which voting 'for communism' is almost impossible to avoid. Turnout invariably exceeds 99 per cent and sometimes reaches 100 per cent. Votes against official candidates tend to add up less than 0.5 per cent of total votes and are mainly cast in elections for local government bodies. Their overall impact is negligible. In the USSR about one candidate in 10,000 fails to be elected, and almost invariably this is at the lowest level of the village Soviet.

The pattern is not fundamentally dissimilar in states with 'limited-choice elections'. Choice is only between personalities and does not extend to policies. All candidates stand on the same official electoral platform and nomination of candidates is still undertaken under the watchful eye of the party. Competition is most common in local government elections and decreases as the importance of the institution rises. For example, in Yugoslavia, where personal electoral competition is most extensive, about 1.5

candidates contest each national legislative seat, and 2.5 candidates each local government seat. Invariably, in all these states, senior or middle-ranking administrative or party office-holders are either returned unopposed or win their 'contested' election comfortably. Turnouts in these states are lower and more unpredictable than in the purely 'plebiscitary' states – as 'low' as 90 per cent in Yugoslavia. Similarly, negative notes cast against all the candidates standing are higher – up to 7 per cent of votes cast in Yugoslavia. Nevertheless, overall, the political impact of these 'limited-choice elections' is very similar to that of their 'plebiscitary' counterparts. In practice they influence the eventual composition of legislative institutions – except at local government level – only very marginally. Furthermore, all direct elections in Second World states relate only to institutions of marginal importance to the making of important political decisions. Consequently such elections not only do not effect *who* rules, but also do not even appear to significantly affect *how* these states are ruled, in terms of any noticeable influence on governmental policies, except, possibly at local government level. Thus the functions of legislative elections in Second World states differ markedly from their First World counterparts with their direct impacts on governmental composition and policies. Their consequent political importance is also markedly less.

Third World regimes
Elections in Third World states likewise do not have the impact of First World national elections, since political groups very frequently do not achieve or retain political power through electoral means. In these states, elections remain only one of several possible strategies open to aspiring political groups, alongside the use of other means of persuasion; coercion – notably and most successfully used by the military but also commonly used by other frustrated social groups; the mobilisation of economic resources – notably by upper-class groups; or the utilisation of technical expertise – principally by the state bureaucracy. Since Third World elections are not the only legitimate and acceptable means of gaining political power, their outcome is never final and the duration of any government which results is always provisional

and uncertain. Moreover, not only are elections only one way in which Third World governments may change hands but they are also almost as frequently non-competitive as those in Second World states. Most of the states of the Third World are of comparatively recent origin with little or no history of electoral competiton either as colonies or since independence. Indeed, independence leaders understandably tended to aim primarily to encourage political unity by seeking mass popular support for a single 'independence' party rather than seeking to encourage open political competition. Once in power it was, and is, inevitable that these same leaders should seek to retain power by discouraging, often by force, the formation and operation of oppositional groupings. Understandably, their successors have tended to play the political game by the same set of rules, and as a result elections tend to have the same limited impact both in conservative authoritarian Third World regimes and in avowedly radical or revolutionary states.

As in the states of the Second World, elections in Third World countries – with a few exceptions which have maintained fully competitive party systems – vary from elections without choice to elections with limited choice. Voters in different states are given varying amounts of freedom to vote for candidates or parties of their choice, and the degree (if any) of limited competition between licensed parties or different candidates from a single party also varies. Similarly the effects which elections have on government policies may also vary quite widely. Most Third World regimes appear to have 'a predilection for unanimity' and many governments utilise coercive means, overtly or covertly, to get the results they want. Nevertheless single-candidate elections without any choice offered to voters are becoming less common, except in presidential ballots.[11] Increasingly, 'one-party' elections in Third World states now consist of competitive ballots between different ruling party candidates. Where this pattern of intra-party competition is well-established, as for example in a number of the states of East Africa, voters certainly may have some influence over the *way* the country is ruled, if not much real choice over *who* rules.

Overall, it must be stressed that the reasons for holding national legislative or presidential elections in Third World states do not tend to include the wish to allow the mass of the people actually to choose their rulers or to exercise any real influence over policy-making. A recent analysis of such 'state-controlled elections' suggests that their political functions are four-fold.[12] First, such elections are an important means of political communication, providing an opportunity for the regime's leaders to attempt to inform their subjects of what the government expects of them. Second, these elections are utilised by ruling groups to attempt to educate their citizens, or rather, and more accurately, to anaesthetise them by offering some limited – if often illusory – participation in the political process. Third, like competitive elections, state-controlled elections are useful to political leaders in their search for legitimacy and as a method of increasing the international acceptability of the regime. Quite simply, elections are held to improve the image of the state and its leadership. Fourth, the holding of elections may be a useful, even necessary, means of settling internal leadership disputes over personnel or policies, and a way of adjusting the distribution of power within the ruling group, or, more commonly, for finally ratifying such adjustments.

Significant political activity in Third World states, to an even greater degree than in Second World states, tends to occur within the confines of a very small ruling group – appropriately referred to by Spaniards as 'the bunker' (on the basis of Hitler's bunker in Berlin in 1945, from which the final Nazi stand was controlled).[13] Variations between states in different geographical regions of what has come to be known as the Third World are often marked. In particular, differences between the more economically developed, longer-established and more highly bureaucratised states in Latin America and their more economically underdeveloped, more recently independent and organisationally and bureaucratically much weaker counterparts in Africa and Asia are very great. Nonetheless the characteristic pattern, outlined in Chapter I, of narrowly based governments whose principal aim and objective is less the pursuit of nationally appropriate developmental policies than the protection of the few who occupy power against the claims of the many who don't, has a very wide applicability to the states of Africa, Asia and Latin America alike.

The characteristic political style of many Third World regimes is one of arbitrary and capricious rule by a small faction or coterie, frequently under-pinning and supporting ultimate control by a single dictatorial figure. Government in such states tends towards personal rule rather than towards institutionalised and regularised forms of government through publicly accepted rules. Politics in such states is literally 'palace' politics.[14] In extreme cases of contemporary tyranny one person effectively becomes the state. Although Central America provided the original model of the 'banana republic' ruled by a succession of dictatorships, Africa has provided its fair share of recent examples of this genre, as the activities of Idi Amin in Uganda, Jean-Badel Bokassa in the Central African Republic, and Macias Nguema in Equatorial Guinea aptly underline. Idi Amin, for example, chillingly explained the fate of missing persons by simply stating that they 'have gone the way of those who foolishly opposed authority.' Macias Nguema – who, in his tiny former Spanish colony, practised genocide on a scale unsurpassed even by the Ugandan ruler – answered a journalist's questioning of his practice of stocking all his state's banknotes in his home village by baldly stating, 'I am the chief of my people, everything belongs to me'. Marshall Bokassa, later self-styled Emperor, at one time combined in his own person the posts of life-president, president of the government, and secretary-general of the ruling and only party, as well as those of the minister of justice, the minister of national defence, war veterans and victims, the minister of public functions and social security, the minister of information, and a general responsibility for the armed forces. John Dunn's comment was apt. 'Beneath the burden of these responsibilities the Marshall plainly had better grounds than even Louis XIV for identifying the state with himself.'[15]

Such ghastly personal tyrannies have most often been confined to the poorest and least developed of the states of the Third World. However they also tend to differ, at least in their decision-making processes, in degree rather than in kind from the general run of governments in these regions – each with their characteristic closed and fortified 'bunker'. In the economically more advanced and politically more developed states of Latin America, for example, the 'bunkers' are characteristically filled by rather larger numbers of politically significant 'notables' than in the newer and poorer states of Africa and Asia, but the basic pattern persists. Even in such a stable and comparatively well-developed state as Mexico the power of the president has been compared to that of the Aztec emperors. 'Personalismo' – personal rule – is the characteristic political style of Latin American presidential government. Thus, in Third World states generally, a small minority rules, often coercively, and dominates the great mass of the population, politically, economically and socially. The potentially wealthy and mineral-rich Central African state of Zaire – widely accepted as the continent's most corrupt country – provides a classical illustration of the pattern and its problems.

Ruled since 1965 by General Mobutu Sese Seko, whose power is absolute, the Zairian 'state' is in the hands of this one man and a few hundred close supporters. Ultimately, access to political power and to wealth and social position depends on a personal relationship with the president. About fifty persons, many related to the president, form what has been termed the 'presidential clique' holding key political and economic positions. Beyond this small tightly-knit circle the remaining key administrative, economic and political posts in the country are in the hands of a few hundred individuals collectively termed the 'reigning brotherhood'. Progressive nationalisation of key economic enterprises, Zairianisation, has allowed those in positions of political and administrative power to become enormously wealthy through corruption, embezzlement and the illegal export of cobalt, coffee, diamonds and ivory. One estimate for 1971, concluded that 60 per cent of state revenue was lost in this way. The wealth of the president alone has been authoritatively estimated at $4–5 billion. At the same time, the national foreign debt stands at $4 billion! Despite its rich natural resources the Zairian economy is in a shambles with all goods, including basic commodities such as food and fuel, in short supply. Both agricultural and industrial production are in decline, inflation runs at close to 100 per cent, and public services such as health and education are deteriorating drastically. Although the world recession and the rising cost of imports, particularly petroleum products, are important factors in this economic decline, government policy and the predatory activities of the political leadership have been equally important contributory factors.

Comparison and its inherent problems: the example of 'authoritarianism'

The contrast between the states of the First World and those of the Second World – in terms of the electoral accountability of the political leadership, and in terms of public influence on the policies as well as on the personnel in government – is marked. The contrast between Third World states and those of the First World is often even more striking. Although few of the world's political leaders can in practice afford to do without elections for long periods (particularly bearing in mind their important international impact), elections are not regularly held in many Third World states. When they are held they frequently tend to be used quite cynically by governments to further entrench themselves in power and to triumphantly demonstrate the extent of their mass support. Thus, from a global perspective, the idea of elections as a choice between different parties with different policies has a relatively limited applicability among contemporary states. This variability in the very meaning as well as in the significance of elections is a useful way of highlighting an inherent danger in comparative studies, namely the problem of ethnocentrism – judging others by one's own standards of behaviour, or literally, according to the Concise Oxford Dictionary, 'Regarding one's own race as the most important'. Comparative studies must inevitably be based on and depart from those experiences most familiar to us – how else could we proceed? However, these experiences should not automatically be taken to be the norm to which others will, or worse should, conform.

For example, despite the fact that the classification of regimes according to the levels of freedom or oppressiveness they achieve – judgements in which differing attitudes to free and competitive elections are an important aspect – has an ancient and honourable pedigree, it still remains highly controversial. Definitions of and beliefs about freedom vary according to ideology. In the contemporary world, 'freedom' is associated with liberty in the states of the First World, where it refers, above all, to the right to choose one's own life without unnecessary state controls. In the Second World states 'freedom' is equated with the absence of social and economic distinctions, and extensive state control is viewed as a necessary method for achieving this egalitarianism. In Third World states, and particularly those most recently independent, 'freedom' tends to refer principally to the achievement of national independence. It is therefore applied to the state's absolute right to self-determination as a sovereign unit and to international rights equal to those of other independent states. Consequently the indexes of political and civil rights – referred to earlier in this chapter – on which First World states rank so highly, must be interpreted and used only with caution. In particular, they must be interpreted with due regard to the existence of cultural and ideological variations in beliefs and behaviour. Non-Western states often explicitly reject Western conceptions of the importance of individual 'human rights' on ideological grounds. Thus in the case of the communist states of the Second World the achievement of social and economic rights – pertaining to groups or classes rather than to individuals, and enforced by the state – is given priority. Alternatively, as evidenced in much of the contemporary Third World, 'human rights' are often viewed as a luxury. Consequently they are given a lower priority as a policy or as a goal than the more immediate demands of economic development and the exigencies of the provision of 'basic needs' such as food and shelter. Nevertheless, the position is clear empirically. From a comparative perspective it is only in the Western First World states that any clear conception of individual rights against the state exists. Moreover it is only in this group of states that individual political and civil rights are regularly protected and enforced to any marked extent. On this empirical basis, these systems – the contemporary liberal democracies of the First World – are characteristically contrasted in the literature of comparative politics with all other contemporary states. The latter are viewed as exhibiting variations on a general theme of authoritarianism.

Authoritarianism – aptly described in a recent comparative analysis as 'rule by the few in the name of the many'[16] – is a blanket term which seeks to describe all those states and regimes which are not competitive democracies. Authoritarian regimes, therefore, are regimes which are not based on free and regular competition for all the most important political offices, or regimes which do not hold elections which are open to all or almost all their citizens. Limitations on the electoral account-ability of the political leadership to the mass public public in such regimes means, in turn, that this leadership – the occupants of the 'bunker' – is able to exercise a far tighter control over political activity than in democratic regimes. Authoritarian regimes seek explicitly to 'subordinate politics' – in particular to reduce or abolish political choice or competition – and 'are char-acterised by repression, intolerance, encroachment on the private rights and freedoms of citizens, and limited autonomy for non-statist interest groups.'[17] Specifically, the ruling group in auth-oritarian regimes seeks to exercise a close control over questions of leadership succession and the composition of the often small and tightly knit political élite in order to ensure that the regime is self-perpetuating.

Accordingly, the borderline between democratic and authori-tarian regimes is a rather clear one. A transition – in either direc-tion – tends to require a decisive, often violent, break and this borderline is seldom crossed by a slow, evolutionary process of change. Authoritarian regimes come to power during crises, and most of these crises involve some violence – ranging from comparatively low levels in many Third World coups to the exceptionally high levels exhibited by such genuinely cataclysmic upheavals as the French, Russian and Chinese revolutions. Conversely, the collapse of an authoritarian regime tends also to require a crisis which is often violent. These crises may be inter-nally stimulated – as in the case of a palace revolt or coup – or externally imposed by war and the active intervention of other states – as in the cases of the fall of Fascist Italy and Nazi Germany. Peaceable transitions from authoritarianism towards democracy are not unknown, but they are less common. They occur when authoritarian leaders conclude that this type of regime no longer meets their own needs, or those of their subjects. The engineered transformation of Turkey from a one-party state into a two-party one in the 1940s, and of Spain from authoritarianism under Franco to constitutional democracy under a restored monarchy in the 1970s, are two classical examples of democratisation under the aegis of previously authoritarian rulers.

Since, by definition, authoritarian rulers will neither willingly surrender nor willingly share political power, authoritarian regimes have developed and utilised distinctive political institutions to secure their control. Some of these characteristic institutions are simply modifications of the same political institutions which are found in the competitive democracies – as in the case of political parties, state bureaucracies and militaries. Other characteristic institutions are more specific to authoritarian systems, notably para-military organisations and a political or secret police. Examples of the former, which are used for achieving and maintaining power, for crushing opposition – whether real, potential or simply imagined – are the Bolshevik's revolutionary Red Guards and Hitler's SA Stormtroops. Typically, such para-military organisations may be destroyed once the regime is secure – as in the case of the SA. Alternatively they may be absorbed into the more conventional political structures of regimes which are typically highly bureaucratised and highly centralised. Nevertheless, established authoritarian regimes tend to retain a powerful political police to ensure continuing political and social conformity. In extreme cases these organisations are of enormous size and great political importance as in the case of the NKVD in Stalinist Russia (now KGB). Here the secret police formed a major political pillar of the regime and had an important, some say a predominant, influence on policy-making.

Clearly, contemporary authoritarian regimes vary one from another – not least in the nature and degree of their authoritarianism. All political institutions – including militaries and bureaucracies – tend to be rudimentary and weak in many of the newly independent states of Asia and Africa. Consequently, no Third World regimes, civilian or military, have achieved and enforced the impressive levels of political centralisation and organisation exhibited by the communist states of the Second World. Institutionally and organisationally, Third World authoritarianism is disorganised and endemically unstable compared to its Second World counterpart. The former regimes have therefore been defined as uninstitutionalised and the latter as institutionalised forms of authoritarianism.[18] Similarly, there are also wide differences of political behaviour and style between Second and Third World authoritarianism, as well as within each of these groups. For example, all authoritarian regimes place restrictions on free political competition and participation, and limit group pluralism, but the nature, extent and effectiveness of these restrictions also vary widely. Some authoritarian regimes – notably Third World military bureaucratic coalitions – demand only public apathy and seek to restrict mass political activity. Others – notably those in the Second World – demand widespread political activity and mass participation and, preferably, widespread enthusiasm in support of governmental policies.

However, whilst it is widely accepted that there is a continuum of authoritarianism – that an individual regime can be more or less authoritarian – no subject in comparative politics has generated such academic heat, and so little consequent light, as the problem of defining and describing these differing degrees or types of authoritarianism. In particular, there has been continuous and fierce controversy among academic writers on politics as to the validity of depicting certain particularly violent, brutal and repressive regimes as 'totalitarian', to distinguish them from other undemocratic but less clearly repressive regimes.

For example the label 'totalitarian' has frequently been used to describe the political system of the USSR, particularly during the Stalinist dictatorship, but also – if less often – in the post-Stalin era. It is universally accepted that the USSR under Stalin was a state based on sustained and systematic repression, which operated for over two decades without any regard for legality and without any respect for human rights or dignity. Although it is impossible to paint an adequate picture of the extent and depth of this repression with statistics alone, some statistics provide illuminating evidence. Some four million people, excluding children, died as a direct or indirect result of the forced collectivisation of agriculture undertaken on Stalin's orders from 1928. Apart from those actually killed, more than one million peasants were placed in prison camps when they resisted these policies. Significantly, Stalin informed Winston Churchill that this period was more stressful even than the Second World War, during which twenty million Soviet citizens died. Moreover, the mass violence of the period of collectivisation was closely followed by the more selective violence of the Great Purge of 1937–8. In this purge, at a minimum tens of thousands and probably more, perhaps far more, of the USSR's political and administrative élite died amidst accusations, by Stalin, of the existence of an anti-Soviet plot. Some estimates claim that millions of Soviet citizens died in this purge, and that up to seven or nine million arrests were made. Whilst these gross figures vary widely, nobody questions the fact that three-quarters of the top one thousand government and party officials, regional leaders, senior military commanders, and factory directors died. Documents captured by the Germans during the Second World War suggest that a total prison camp population of just under seven million existed in the USSR in 1941. It has been estimated that a total of twelve million Soviet citizens died in these prison camps – run by the secret police – between 1936 and 1950.[19]

Whilst this systematic use and threat of mass terror was only one aspect of the Stalinist personal dictatorship, it was the central pillar of his governmental methods, and has aptly been described as forming a 'persistent regime of terror'.[20] Significantly, this style of rule did not survive the death of the dictator: since Stalin's death, the USSR has been transformed from a personal dictatorship into an oligarchical system in which leadership and decision-making has increasingly become a collective rather than an individual activity. Each successive general secretary appears to have possessed less individual power over policy-making than his predecessor. It is reported that Leonid Brezhnev told a senior Czech politician in 1968, that 'perhaps I can manage about one-third of what I'd like to do.' Stalin, on the other hand, was personally able to decide anything he wanted to, without any constraints placed on him by any individuals, groups, organisations or laws. 'He would just make a decision,' stated Khrushchev, 'and issue a decree.'[21] This passing of personal dictatorship has been accompanied by the disappearance of mass political terror, the closure of most of the prison camps and by a decline in the size and political importance of the secret police, on whom Stalin had relied so heavily to enforce his will. Moreover, whilst the increasingly 'collective' rather than individual nature of the political leadership, and an absence of terror by no means exhausts the list of major post-Stalin changes, they do graphically underline the existence of a much-changed style of regime.

Nevertheless, dissent is still firmly and often forcibly repressed in the contemporary USSR. 'Dissidents' are arbitrarily imprisoned, exiled internally, expelled from the country or incarcerated in psychiatric institutions as insane. The average Soviet citizen is deprived of fundamental freedoms of speech, association and movement in comparison to his Western counterpart. Individuals still lack any effective legal remedies against state actions and administrative abuse of power. Not surprisingly, 'authoritarian' is the term most commonly used to describe this increasingly 'conservative and limited repressive regime'.[22] Equally unsurprisingly, relatively few scholars consider that the contemporary Soviet Union can be described as totalitarian. It may, however, come as more of a surprise to learn that many scholars now refuse to use the word totalitarian in labelling the USSR at all – even under Stalin. This refusal is not an outcome of a desire to rehabilitate, excuse, forget, or explain away the excesses and horrors of that era in Soviet history. It simply reflects the failure of scholars to agree on the features that constitute totalitarianism, and, therefore, on what exactly that concept seeks to highlight and to categorise. Thus, one author, who surveyed the literature in the late 1960s, quotes thirteen different definitions of this one concept, and found it applied to an equally diverse group of contemporary and historical states.[23]

If such a survey were to be conducted again today, many additional definitions of totalitarianism could be added. Since this search for a generally acceptable definition has now continued for over thirty-five years without any real agreement or consensus emerging among authors – who all tend to believe that their definition is the most apt – the concept has now been abandoned by many comparativists, often in favour of the wider, but obviously vaguer term, 'authoritarianism'. Yet the basic problem remains – how best to describe and categorise the varying forms taken, and the different degrees of intensity exhibited, by authoritarian regimes, either among different states, or, as in the case of the USSR, in one state as it changes over time? Thus the original problem which has sustained scholarly debate over the nature and validity of the concept of totalitarianism remains unsolved. Indeed this particular problem is but one instance of the basic, the perennial, problem underlying all comparative political enquiry – how best to categorise, classify and generalise about political phenomena on the basis of observed similarities and differences.

Notes and References

Chapter 1. Contemporary Regimes: An Introductory Classification

1. These phrases were used by Ivo D. Duchachek & Herman Finer respectively. See Ivo D. Duchachek, *Power Maps: Comparative Politics of Constitutions* (Santa Barbara, Clio Press, 1973). Herman Finer, *The Theory and Practice of Modern Government* 4th ed, (Methuen, 1961).

2. Douglas E. Ashford, 'The Structural Analysis of Policy: Or Institutions Really Do Matter', in Ashford ed, *Comparing Public Policies: New Concepts and Methods* (Beverly Hills, Sage Publications Inc, 1978), pp. 81–98, p. 86.

3. These studies are analysed and brought up-to-date in G. Bingham Powell, Jr, *Contemporary Democracies: Participation, Stability and Violence* (Harvard University Press, 1982).

4. *Ibid*, p. 238, fn 3.

5. Michael Waller, 'The Communist Movement: From Monolith to Polymorph', in Bogdan Szajkowski ed, *Marxist Governments: A World Survey* Vol 1 (Macmillan, 1981), pp. 1–19, p. 17.

6. Stephen White, 'What is a Communist System?' Paper given at Political Studies Association Annual Conference, Newcastle-upon-Tyne, 1983, p. 6.

7. Stephen White, John Gardner and George Schöpflin, *Communist Political Systems: An Introduction* (Macmillan, 1982), pp. 3–4.

8. eg in Peter Wiles ed, *The New Communist Third World* (Croom Helm, 1982).

9. This account closely follows Robert Rothstein, *The Weak in the World of the Strong: The Developing Countries in the International System* (Columbia University Press, 1977), esp Ch 6 'Politics and Policymaking: Problems and Prospects'. See also, *Handbook of World Development: The Guide to the Brandt Report*, compiled by G J W Government Relations with Peter Stephenson, (Longman, 1981).

10. Robert H Jackson and Carl G Rosberg, *Personal Rule in Black Africa: Prince, Autocrat, Prophet, Tyrant* (University of California Press, 1982), p. 18.

11. Dennis Austin, *Politics in Africa* (Manchester University Press, 1978), p. 28. Emphasis in original.

12. Karl W Deutsch, Jorge I Dominguez, and Hugh Heclo, *Comparative Government: Politics of Industrialized and Developing Nations* (Houghton Mifflin, 1981), p. 6.

Chapter 2. Political Leadership: Executives in the Modern World

1. Anthony King, 'Executives', in Fred I. Greenstein and Nelson W. Polsby eds, *Handbook of Political Science* Vol 5, (Addison-Wesley Publishing Company, 1975), pp. 173–256.
2. *Ibid*, p. 181.
3. *Ibid*, p. 182.
4. Jean Blondel, *The Organization of Governments: A Comparative Analysis of Governmental Structures* (Sage Publications Ltd, 1982), p. 206.
5. Jean Blondel, *World Leaders: Heads of Government in the Postwar Period* (Sage Publications Ltd, 1980), p. 21.
6. *Ibid*, p. 56.
7. James Madison, *The Federalist* No 51, quoted in William J. Keefe et al, *American Democracy: Institutions, Politics, and Policies* (Homewood, Illinois, The Dorsey Press, 1983), p. 26.
8. Richard E. Neustadt, *Presidential Power: The Politics of Leadership from FDR to Carter* (John Wiley & Sons, Inc, 2nd ed, 1980), p. 26.
9. Blondel, *World Leaders, op cit*, pp. 59–60.
10. This was the conclusion of the President's Committee on Administrative Management (1937), always known by the name of its chairman, Louis Brownlow.
11. Neustadt, *op cit*, passim.
12. H. Heclo, *A Government of Strangers* (Washington, The Brookings Institution, 1977).
13. Keefe et al, *op cit*, p. 351.
14. Alan Grant, *The American Political Process* (Heinemann, 2nd ed, 1982), p. 104.
15. Blondel, *The Organization of Governments, op cit*, p. 83.

Chapter 3. Contemporary Legislatures

1. R. Hague and M. Harrop, *Comparative Government: An Introduction* (Macmillan, 1982), p. 133.
2. J. Blondel, *Comparative Legislatures* (Prentice-Hall, 1973), pp. 7–9.
3. Gerhard Loewenberg and Samuel C. Patterson, *Comparing Legislatures* (Little, Brown & Co, 1979), p. 233.
4. *Ibid*, p. 277.
5. Michael L. Mezey, *Comparative Legislatures* (Duke University Press, 1979), pp. 25–26.
6. Blondel, *op cit*, p. 8.
7. *Ibid*, p. 135.
8. Mezey, *op cit*, p. 36.

9. Loewenberg & Patterson, *op cit*, p. 182.
10. Stephen White, 'The USSR Supreme Soviet: A Developmental Perspective', in Daniel Nelson and Stephen White, eds, *Communist Legislatures in Comparative Perspective* (Macmillan, 1982) p. 134.
11. Quoted in *ibid*, p. 134.
12. *Ibid*, p. 153.
13. This is Stephen White's balanced conclusion. *Ibid*, pp. 126–127.
14. James L. Sundquist, *The Decline and Resurgence of Congress* (The Brookings Institution, 1981), p. 418.
15. Cited in *ibid*, p. 447.
16. Quoted in John Spanier and Joseph Nogee, eds. *Congress, The Presidency and American Foreign Policy* (Pergamon, 1981) pp. 191–192.
17. Sundquist, *op cit*, p. 406.
18. Thomas E. Mann and Norman J. Ornstein, eds, *The New Congress* (American Enterprise Institute for Public Policy Research, 1981), p. 381.

Chapter 4. Political Centralisation and Decentralisation: The Nature of Federalism and Federal Government

1. Martin Kolinsky, 'The Nation-State in Western Europe: Erosion from "Above" and "Below"?', in L. Tivey, ed, *The Nation-State: The Formation of Modern Politics* (Martin Robertson, 1981), pp. 82–103.
2. The two definitions are from W. H. Riker, 'Federalism', in F. I. Greenstein and N. Polsby, eds, Vol 5, *op cit*, pp 93–172, p 101, and from G. Bingham Powell, Jr, *op cit*, p. 270, fn. 9, respectively.
3. U. K. Hicks, *Federalism: Failure and Success, A Comparative Study* (Macmillan, 1978), p. 171.

Chapter 5. Parties and Party Systems

1. S. P. Huntington, *Political Order in Changing Societies* (Yale University Press, 1968), p. 90.
2. G. Sartori, *Parties and Party Systems* (Cambridge University Press, 1976), p 64.
3. R. Rose, 'The Variability of Party Government', *Political Studies*, 17, 4, December 1969, pp. 413–445, p. 414.
4. Figures from J. Blondel, *The Organization of Governments* (*op cit*), pp. 97–101.
5. Kay Lawson, *The Comparative Study of Political Parties* (St Martin's Press, 1976), p 18. M. Duverger, *Political Parties*, translated by B. and R. North, 2nd ed, (Methuen, 1959).
6. Vernon Bogdanor 'Introduction' in V. Bogdanor and D. Butler,

eds, *Democracy and Elections: Electoral Systems and their Political Consequences* (Cambridge University Press, 1983), pp. 1–19, p. 1.

7. Vernon Bogdanor, 'Conclusion: Electoral Systems and Party Systems', in *Ibid* pp. 247–262, p. 251.

8. R. Michels, *Political Parties*, translated by E. and C. Paul, (The Free Press, 1962), p. 15.

9. Lawson, *op cit*, p. 78.

10. Quoted in *ibid*, p. 210, fn. 1.

11. *Ibid*, p 137.

12. Jean Charlot, *The Gaullist Phenomenon*, translated by M Charlot and M Neighbour, (George Allen & Unwin, 1971), p. 43.

13. Bogdanor, 'Conclusion', *op cit*, p. 261.

14. Hugh Bone and Clinton Rossiter are quoted in K. Janda, 'A Comparative Analysis of Party Organizations', in William Crotty, ed, *The Party Symbol: Readings on Political Parties* (San Francisco, W H Freeman & Co, 1980), pp. 339–358, p. 346, and p. 347 respectively.

15. J. McGinniss, *The Selling of the President, 1968* (New York, Trident Press, 1969).

16. J. D. Lees, R. A. Maidment and M. Tappin, *American Politics Today* (Manchester University Press, 1982), p. 89.

17. R. J. Hill and P. Frank, *The Soviet Communist Party* 2nd ed, (George Allen & Unwin, 1983), p. 1.

18. Quoted in *ibid*, p. 2.

19. *Ibid*, p. 70.

20. John Löwenhardt, *The Soviet Politburo*, translated by D. Clark, (Edinburgh, Canongate Publishing Ltd, 1982), pp. 102–104.

21. J. F. Hough and M. Fainsod, *How the Soviet Union is Governed* (Harvard University Press, 1979), p. 423.

22. Lawson, *op cit*, p. 235.

Chapter 6. Pressure Groups in the Political Process

1. Gordon B. Smith, 'Bureaucratic Politics and Public Policy in the Soviet Union', in Gordon B. Smith ed, *Public Policy and Administration in the Soviet Union* (Praeger, 1980), pp. 1–17, p. 4.

2. R. Furtak cited in H. G. Skilling, 'Interest Groups and Communist Politics Revisited', *World Politics*, XXXVI, 1, Oct 1983, pp. 1–27, pp. 19–20.

3. H. J. Wiarda and H. F. Kline eds, *Latin American Politics and Development* (Boston, Houghton Mifflin Co, 1979), pp. 41–56.

4. G. Lehmbruch, 'Introduction: Neo-Corporatism in Comparative Perspective' in G. Lehmbruch and P. C. Schmitter eds, *Patterns*

196   Notes and References

of Corporatist Policy-Making (Sage Publications Ltd, 1982), p 1–28, pp 16–25.

5. T. J. Pempel and K. Tsunekawa, 'Corporatism without Labour? The Japanese Anomaly', in P. Schmitter and G. Lehmbruch eds, *Trends Toward Corporatist Intermediation* (Sage Publications Ltd, 1979), pp. 231–270.

6. G. K. Wilson, *Interest Groups in the United States* (Oxford, Clarendon Press, 1981).

7. Cited in *ibid*, p. 130.

8. Cited in *ibid*, p. 55.

9. *Ibid*, p. 4.

10. *Ibid*, p. 138.

11. *Ibid*, p. 81.

12. J. F. Hough and M. Fainsod, *op cit*, p 387.

13. All terms cited in S. G. Solomon, ed, *Pluralism in the Soviet Union* (The Macmillan Press Ltd, 1983).

14. Archie Brown, 'Pluralism, Power and the Soviet Political System: A Comparative Perspective', in *ibid*, pp. 61–107, and pp. 72–73.

15. *Ibid*, p. 79.

16. Cited in Skilling, *op cit*, p. 9.

17. *Ibid*, p. 9.

18. D. R. Kelley, 'Environmental Policy-Making in the USSR: The Role of Industrial and Environmental Interest Groups', *Soviet Studies*, 28, 1976, pp 570–589

19. Quoted in Hill and Frank, *op cit*, p. 14.

20. Skilling, *op cit*, p. 23.

21. Brown, *op cit*, p. 77 and p. 95.

Chapter 7. Contemporary Civilian Bureaucracies

1. Edward Feit, *The Armed Bureaucrats: Military-Administrative Regimes and Political Development* (Houghton Mifflin Co, 1973).

2. J. Blondel, *The Discipline of Politics* (Butterworth, 1981), p. 52.

3. Alec Nove, cited in A. H. Brown, *Soviet Politics and Political Science* (Macmillan, 1974), p. 69. Alfred Meyer, cited in White, Gardner and Schöpflin, *op cit*, p. 21.

4. B. Guy Peters, *The Politics of Bureaucracy: A Comparative Perspective* (Longman, 1978), pp. 92–93.

5. Quoted in Hague and Harrop, *op cit*, p. 201.

6. Peters, *op cit*, pp. 218–219.

7. *Ibid*, pp. 207–209.

8. Vincent Wright, *The Government and Politics of France*, 2nd ed (Hutchinson, 1983), p. 124.

9. Quoted in R. H. W. Theen, 'Party and Bureaucracy', in Gordon B. Smith, ed, *op cit*, pp. 18–52, p. 46.
10. Hough and Fainsod, *op cit*, pp. 383–386.
11. Quoted in Peters, *op cit*, p. 160.
12. Peter H Smith, quoted in Susan Kaufman Purcell, 'Mexico: Clientalism, Corporatism and Political Stability', in S. N. Eisenstadt and R. Lemarchand, eds, *Political Clientalism, Patronage and Development* (Sage Publications, 1981) pp. 191–216, p. 202.
13. Quoted in Colin Leys, *Underdevelopment in Kenya: The Political Economy of Neo-Colonialism, 1964–1971* (Heinemann, 1975), p. 193.

Chapter 8. Politics and the Military: the 'Armed Bureaucrats'

1. S. E. Finer, *The Man on Horseback: The Role of the Military in Politics*, 2nd ed (Penguin Books Ltd, 1976), p. 5.
2. Eric A. Nordlinger, *Soldiers in Politics: Military Coups and Governments* (Prentice-Hall Inc, 1977), p. 6.
3. *Ibid*, pp. 12–19. S. P. Huntington, *The Soldier and the State: The Theory and Politics of Civil-Military Relations* (Harvard University Press, 1957), Chapter 4.
4. Quoted in Nordlinger, *op cit*, p. 16.
5. *Khrushchev Remembers*, translated by Strobe Talbot, (Sphere Books Ltd, 1971), pp. 474–475. *Khrushchev Memoirs*, quoted in *The Times*, 11 May 1974, p. 5. President Eisenhower quoted in Douglass Cater, *Power in Washington* (Collins, 1965), p. 26.
6. Ron Huisken, 'Estimating Soviet Military Expenditure', in Philip Towle, ed, *Estimating Foreign Military Power* (Croom Helm, 1982), pp. 77–87. ACDA, *World Military Expenditures and Arms Transfers, 1969–1978*, Washington, 1980.
7. *Krushchev Memoirs*, *op cit*, p. 5. Brezhnev quoted in Timothy J. Colton, *Commissars, Commanders, and Civilian Authority* (Harvard University Press, 1979), p. 284.
8. Nordlinger, *op cit*, p. 109.
9. S. E. Finer, 'The Morphology of Military Regimes', in Roman Kolkowicz and Andrzej Korbonski, eds, *Soldiers, Peasants, and Bureaucrats* (George Allen & Unwin, 1982), pp. 281–309, p. 283.
10. E. Luttwak, *Coup d'Etat: A Practical Handbook*, 2nd ed (Wildwood House, 1979).
11. Quoted in Colton, *op cit*, p. 282.
12. M. Janowitz, *The Military in the Political Development of New Nations* (University of Chicago Press, 1964), p. 65.
13. Quoted in Nordlinger, *op cit*, p. 113.

Chapter 9. Conclusion: Regimes Revisited

1. G. Bingham Powell, *op cit*, p. 182.
2. Robert A Dahl, *Dilemmas of Pluralist Democracy: Autonomy vs Control* (Yale University Press, 1982), p. 26.
3. *Ibid*, pp. 28–29.
4. Hill and Frank, *op cit*, p. 148. Quotations from Ilyichev and Brezhnev are cited in Aryeh L. Unger, *The Totalitarian Party: Party and People in Nazi Germany and Soviet Russia* (Cambridge University Press, 1974), p. 65.
5. Quotation in Hill and Frank, *op cit*, pp. 12–13 and p. 4.
6. Jerry F. Hough, *Soviet Leadership in Transition* (The Brookings Institution, 1980), p. 76.
7. Robert V. Daniels, quoted in *ibid*, p. 77.
8. Archie Brown, 'The Soviet Succession: From Andropov to Chernenko', *The World Today*, 40, 4, April 1984, pp. 134–141, p. 134.
9. G. Hermet, R. Rose, and A. Rouquié, *Elections Without Choice* (The Macmillan Press Ltd, 1978).
10. Alex Pravda, 'Elections in Communist Party States', in *ibid*, pp. 169–195, p. 172.
11. Guy Hermet, 'State-Controlled Elections: A Framework', *in ibid*, pp. 1–18, p. 7.
12. *Ibid*, pp. 13–17.
13. *Ibid*, p. 9.
14. On 'palace' politics see Bernard Crick, *In Defence of Politics* (Penguin Books Ltd, 1964), pp. 20–24.
15. Idi Amin, quoted in D. Austin, *op cit*, p. 31. Macias Nguema, quoted in J-F. Medard, 'The Underdeveloped State in Tropical Africa', in C. Clapham ed, *Private Patronage and Public Power: Political Clientelism in the Modern State* (London, Frances Pinter, 1982), pp. 162–192, p. 186. John Dunn, 'Comparing West African States', in John Dunn ed, *West African States: Failure and Promise* (Cambridge University Press, 1978), pp. 1–21, p. 3.
16. Amos Perlmutter, *Modern Authoritarianism: A Comparative Institutional Analysis* (Yale University Press, 1981), p. 2.
17. *Ibid*, pp. 7–8.
18. *Ibid*, p. 5.
19. Figures quoted in Seweryn Bialer, *Stalin's Successors: Leadership, Stability and Change in the Soviet Union* (Cambridge University Press, 1980), p. 13, fn. 16, pp. 59–60, in Hough, *op cit*, pp. 38–40, and in Hough and Fainsod, *op cit*, pp. 176–177.
20. Bialer, *op cit*, p. 14.
21. Brezhnev and Khrushchev quoted in Archie Brown, 'The Power

of the General Secretary of the CPSU', in T. H. Rigby, Archie Brown and Peter Reddaway, eds, *Authority, Power and Policy in the USSR* (Macmillan, 1980), pp. 135–157, p. 144.

22. Hough, *op cit*, p. 4.

23. Benjamin R. Barber, 'Conceptual Foundations of Totalitarianism', in C. J. Friederich, M. Curtis, and B. R. Barber, eds, *Totalitarianism in Perspective: Three Views* (Praeger, 1969), pp. 3–52, pp. 7–10.

Further Reading

The references given in the individual chapters should be regarded as the starting point for further reading in all the areas covered by this book. Accordingly this short list of further reading simply seeks to suggest a few additional titles as yet unmentioned, and to underline the importance of one or two already cited.

Despite the ever-growing literature in the field of comparative politics goods introductory texts are rare. Among older works, S. E. Finer, *Comparative Government* (Penguin Books Ltd, 1974), and Jean Blondel, *An Introduction to Comparative Government* (Weidenfeld & Nicolson, 1969) remain useful. Among newer texts, Rod Hague and Martin Harrop, *Comparative Government: An Introduction* (The Macmillan Press Ltd, 1982) is clearly written and provides an excellent introduction to the subject.

Works of reference are indispensable to those who wish to keep up to date in such a vast and ever-changing field. Here *Keesing's Contemporary Archives* proves particularly useful with its comprehensive, and very reliable, global coverage, and its comparatively simple referencing system. Alan J. Day and Henry W. Degenhardt eds, *Political Parties of the World* (Longman, 2nd ed, 1984) is a mine of useful information. So too is the *Handbook of World Development: The Guide to the Brandt Report* (compiled by GJW Government Relations with Peter Stephenson, Longman, 1981).

The publication of Christopher Clapham's *Third World Politics: An Introduction* (Croom Helm, 1985) has very satisfactorily filled one of the most glaring of the gaps in comparative politics literature – the absence of a good introductory text on Third World politics. Further comparative studies of both modern liberal democracies and modern dictatorships – as opposed to studies of modern democracy and modern dictatorship – would be very useful. Samuel P Huntington's 'Will More Countries Become Democratic?' (*Political Science Quarterly*, 99, 2, Summer 1984, pp. 193–218) both asks an important question and provides a brief and readable synthesis of the literature to date.

Finally, historical dimensions are introduced in Samuel E. Finer, 'Perspectives in the World History of Government – a Prolegomenon' (*Government and Opposition*, 18, 1, Winter 1983, pp. 3–22). Bernard Crick, *Basic Forms of Government: A Sketch and a Model* (The Macmillan Press Ltd, 1973) outlines an historically-based classification.

Index

Countries

Afghanistan, 1
Australia, 62
Austria, 57

Bangladesh, 60
Belgium, 60
Brazil, 165

Cameroon, 60
Canada, 53, 62
Central African Republic, 21–22
Chile, 7, 131
China, 10, 153, 155
Colombia, 22
Costa Rica, 22, 40, 151
Cuba, 10
Czechoslovakia, 27, 108, 171

East Germany, 27
Egypt, 60
Ethiopia, 11, 103

France, 6, 28, 33–34, 73, 106,
    129–130, 136, 139–140, 141,
    152–153, 169

Germany, 77, 78
Ghana, 7, 25, 147, 164–165, 166
Greece, 7, 75, 152
Guinea-Bissau, 130

India, 7, 24, 62, 78, 98
Iran, 11
Italy, 40, 77, 112, 169

Jamaica, 7
Japan, 78, 115, 169
Jordan, 159

Kampuchea, 10
Kenya, 43, 130, 150

Laos, 10
Lesotho, 130
Liberia, 11, 76
Libya, 60

Mauritius, 98–99
Mexico, 21, 62, 98, 148–149
Morocco, 60, 159

Nigeria, 7, 60, 131, 165, 166
North Korea, 10

Pakistan, 60, 147–148
Philippines, 159–160
Poland, 75, 104, 108, 109, 153, 171
Portugal, 7, 75, 77, 152

Senegambia, 60
Spain, 7, 75, 77, 153, 186–187
Sri Lanka (Ceylon), 7
Sudan, 60
Sweden, 138
Switzerland, 25, 57

Thailand, 11
Turkey, 7, 11, 186–187

United Arab Emirates, 60
United Kingdom, 24, 43, 52, 56–57,
    79–80, 82, 84, 87, 102, 114, 115,
    134–135, 138–139
Uruguay, 7, 25
USA, bureaucracy in, 141–143, and,
    executive in, 27, 35–37
    federalism in, 63–67
    legislature in, 49–54
    military in, 155, 157
    parties in, 84–89
    presidency in, 33–37
    pressure groups in, 116–123
USSR, bureaucracy in, 144–146,
    and,
    CPSU, 72, 76, 89–97

201

Names

Subjects

Acknowledgements

Cover photographs by Camera Press (below); J. Allan Cash (above); United States Travel Service (centre).